IS GOD A MISOGYNIST?

UNDERSTANDING THE BIBLE'S DIFFICULT PASSAGES CONCERNING WOMEN

DAVID WILBER

David Wilber
www.davidwilber.me

In his book, *Is God A Misogynist?*, Wilber's direct and to-the-point approach makes this a must-have companion for any church pastoral staff, teacher, or even layperson. Wilber's ability to confront objections to the Bible regarding the topics of gender, sex, and marriage with well-articulated arguments equips the reader to defend the text with a clear understanding. I genuinely think this is not only an edifying work but also an essential resource for any believer in this day and age.

—**Matthew Vander Els**, Founded in Truth

Modern feminists, through a faulty interpretation of select biblical passages, regularly and relentlessly paint the Christian faith as part of the problem in the scope of gender inequality. In his book, Wilber not only brilliantly exposes such interpretive error but also demonstrates how the Bible is the most ancient source that actually promotes gender rights and equality. Wilber's book is a refreshing relief from the common confusion that is often thoughtlessly regurgitated in modern feminist circles.

—**Jon Sherman**, 119 Ministries

This book is a great tool to use when you are confronted with the claim that Christianity is a misogynistic religion. David addresses any verse a critic could bring up and provides you with valuable context that demonstrates the Bible actually promotes equality and respect for women. If you want to study the biblical view of women, this book is a great place to start.

—**Michael Jones**, Inspiring Philosophy

Amidst the ever-evolving cultural perception of a woman's value, it is imperative that we know who is truly championing the cause—Christianity or modern, secular feminism? David Wilber delivers a carefully substantiated, biblically secure resource demonstrating the God of Israel's advocacy for women.

—**Matt Hoffmann**, Freedom Hill Community

The history of women within both Judaism and Christianity was meant by our God to be joyful, dignified, and fulfilling. Sadly, too many men, ignorant of the historical context of Scripture and imprisoned by the prejudices of their day, have read their own worldviews into the text and recreated God and the Bible in their own image. Modern feminism, rooted in much pain and anger, is the unintended yet inevitable consequence of a system that has perpetuated one of the results of the fall—man's domination over women instead of the originally designed partnership—as an ideal to be legalistically lived out instead of just one more curse "finished" at the Cross. It is my prayer that David's book will reach deep into some damaged souls and reveal the tender love of God to those who have inadvertently been laboring against Him on both sides.

—**Tyler Dawn Rosenquist**, Author of *Sexuality, Social Identity and Kinship Relations in the Bible*

IS GOD A
MISOGYNIST?

UNDERSTANDING THE BIBLE'S DIFFICULT PASSAGES CONCERNING WOMEN

DAVID WILBER

CONTENTS

AUTHOR'S PREFACE

Being a follower of Yeshua[1] includes the task of developing sound theology in accordance with the Scriptures. Since theology, by definition, is "the study of God" and involves seeking to know God as He has revealed Himself, every Christian is technically a theologian. Even if someone says they don't care about theology but only about "loving people" (whatever that means to them) because "that's all God really cares about," they are still engaging in theology. They are attempting to explain what God is like according to how they think He has revealed Himself. The only question is whether or not their theology is any good. The idea that God wants us to have only a shallow understanding of His revelation is not good theology. It also doesn't help us love people.

Why is developing sound theology so important? Beyond the fact that the greatest commandment is to love the Lord with all our heart, soul, and mind (Matthew 22:37), and the only way to do that is to study the Scriptures so we can learn what it means to love Him, there are many reasons. A big reason is that our beliefs fuel our behavior and ministry to others. Thus, a shallow theology produces a shallow church that fails to meet the intellectual needs of the people. For instance, the Scriptures instruct us to "have mercy on those who doubt" (Jude 22). That is, the

---

1   Throughout this book I will be referring to Jesus by His Hebrew name, Yeshua, except when I quote other sources.

Church is called to minister to the doubtful in our communities. That means providing a safe environment for those who have doubts about the Scriptures to wrestle with difficult questions while guiding them and working with them to find answers. We must make sure we are established in our faith (Jude 20-21) so that we can effectively minister to those in our community who struggle with doubt. That requires us to be equipped in apologetics, which is a branch of theology devoted to defending Christianity's truth claims.

Many people have abandoned Christianity—or they've embraced some hyper-liberal version of Christianity that rejects the authority and divine inspiration of Scripture (but I repeat myself)—because they've come to believe that the Bible contains serious moral problems. These concerns deserve answers. Unfortunately, too many pastors and leaders are unprepared (or unwilling) to address these types of matters. As a result, many serious inquirers are left to conclude that some issues are irreconcilable, and thus the Bible must be rejected because of its apparent problematic teaching. This scenario could perhaps be avoided if more believers were equipped to address challenges to the Bible with grace, wisdom, and intelligence.

One reason that many men and women have walked away from their faith (including a few people I know personally) is that they've come to believe the Bible contains misogynistic teachings. Swayed by feminist rhetoric, many have come to view the Bible—the Old Testament, in particular, but also some passages in the New Testament—as being hopelessly sexist and oppressive toward women. When the concerns of these people are met with overly-simplistic and poorly researched answers from Christians, it only reinforces this misperception about the Scriptures. Seeing people walk away from Christianity over such concerns has inspired me to write this book.

I have three goals with this book: first, to prepare believers with answers they can give to those who raise these particular objections to the Scriptures (1 Peter 3:15). Second, to provide a correct biblical perspective to those who struggle over difficult passages concerning women. Third, to correct common false doctrines and viewpoints regarding women, which have contributed to bad theology and practice in the Church. My prayer is that people will find hope in what the Bible actually teaches when these issues are examined thoughtfully and in context, and that they will be encouraged by the fact that God has revealed Himself to be a God who loves women and is especially concerned for their welfare. Indeed, women have immense value and purpose, just like men, and nowhere in the Scriptures has God revealed that women are inferior to men in His eyes.

May you find this book to be a blessing as you study this important topic. Shalom in the matchless name of Yeshua the Messiah!

CHAPTER 1
GOD'S PERSPECTIVE
ON WOMEN

Critics of Christianity often claim that the Bible contains misogynistic teachings—that is, instructions expressing an inherent prejudice against women. Some say that the Bible regards women as unclean, less valuable than men, and mere property to be bought and sold.[1] Some have argued that religions such as Christianity are "the last cultural barrier to gender equality."[2] Some say that God—if He exists—could not have inspired the Bible because of its "sexist" message.[3] Others even go so far as to say that feminism and atheism have a "moral obligation" to be vocal about the supposed misogyny of the Bible, and that the only way toward human progress and cultural protection for women is to abandon religion.[4]

---

1   See Karen Garst, "Introduction," *Women V. Religion: The Case Against Faith—and for Freedom.* Karen L. Garst, ed. (Durham, NC: Pitchstone Publishing, 2018): "All of the Abrahamic religions originally subjugated women, making them less worthy than men, unable to participate in religious leadership, and even responsible for original sin. Women were considered property and could be bought and sold like slaves and killed for committing adultery or for not being virgins when they married. They couldn't own property and were considered unclean." (p. 14)

2   Ibid., p. 13

3   See Karen Garst, *Faithless Feminist.* "Ten Reasons for Women to Reject Christianity." www.faithlessfeminist.com. Accessed 9/16/19: "[The story of Genesis] is not sacred or the inspired word of a deity, because it was written by men who believed women were their property."

4   See Lauri Weissman, "Half Human: How Jewish Law Justifies the Exclusion and Exploitation of Women," *Women V. Religion: The Case Against Faith—and for Freedom.* Karen L. Garst, ed. (Durham, NC: Pitchstone Publishing, 2018): "Vocal feminism and atheism now are moral obligations: anything less makes us complicit in the

Are the critics right about Christianity being bad for women? Would women be better off if we all became atheists? What does the Bible actually teach about the value and personhood of women?

Before we zero in on some of the Bible's difficult passages that appear, on the surface, to denigrate women, let's broadly establish God's perspective as revealed in Scripture. The overall message of the Bible affirms the immense value and personhood of women, which is equal to that of men. This perspective is evident in the very beginning of the biblical narrative:

> So God created man in his own image, in the image of God
> he created him; **male and female he created them.** (Genesis
> 1:27, emphasis added)

Here we see that God created both men and women in His image. Being created in God's image not only bestows upon humans intrinsic value but also elects them to represent God's purposes and will on earth.[5] That is, both men and women are equal in dignity and vocation in God's creation and plan.[6] Feminism doesn't get the credit for the concept that women have equal value; the Bible taught this concept first.

---

dehumanization, commoditization, and sexual exploitation of women. To protect the defenseless and progress toward humanism, women must abandon religion." (p. 72)

5   See J. Richard Middleton, *The Liberating Image: The Imago Dei in Genesis 1* (Grand Rapids, MI: Brazos Press, 2005): "…careful exegesis of Genesis 1:26-28, in conjunction with an intertextual reading of the symbolic world of Genesis 1, does indeed suggest that the *imago Dei* refers to human rule, that is, the exercise of power on God's behalf in creation." (p. 88)

6   This is not at all to diminish the important *differences* between men and women in regard to their biology, their unique God-given perspectives, strengths, needs and desires, etc., which ought to be appreciated and celebrated.

This immediately raises a question: if the Bible was hopelessly misogynistic, as some claim, why do women share the special status of bearing God's image along with men? If the Bible presented women as being inferior to men, wouldn't we expect God to make that clear from the beginning? Wouldn't we expect the Scriptures to declare women to be on the same level as animals? Instead, Scripture teaches that women, just like men, have inherent value and purpose. Women even share with men the blessing of dominion over creation (Genesis 1:28). As Dr. Richard Davidson writes, "The fundamental equality of man and woman is unhesitatingly proclaimed in the first chapter of the Bible."[7]

This is further confirmed when we look at the creation of Eve:

> So the Lord God caused a deep sleep to fall upon the man, and
> while he slept took one of his ribs and closed up its place with
> flesh. And the rib that the Lord God had taken from the man
> he made into a woman and brought her to the man. Then the
> man said, "This at last is bone of my bones and flesh of my
> flesh; she shall be called Woman, because she was taken out of
> Man." (Genesis 2:21-23)

The Hebrew word for the man's "rib" in this passage is *tsela*, which means "side." This word typically means the entire side of something, such as the side of the Ark or the side of a hill (Exodus 25:14; 1 Samuel 16:13). Thus, Eve is represented as Adam's "other half," if you will. Adam is incomplete without her by his side: "It is not good that the man should be alone" (Genesis 2:18). Adam needed a partner to fulfill

---

7   Richard M. Davidson, *Flame of Yahweh: Sexuality in the Old Testament* (Peabody, MA: Hendrickson Publishers, 2007), p. 22

the divine calling of subduing and ruling over creation, being fruitful and filling the earth (Genesis 1:28), and working and keeping the Garden—that is, serving as types of priests tasked with caring for sacred space[8] (Genesis 2:15). Men and women are created to work together to fulfill God's purposes. Indeed, when he sees the woman for the first time, Adam poetically exclaims, "This at last is bone of my bones and flesh of my flesh," which is a statement that emphasizes "the similarities, and the intended bond and partnership, that Adam was to have with his wife Eve."[9]

Therefore, this passage confirms once again the ontological equality of man and woman. While men and women are certainly created with important differences, as human creatures who bear God's image, neither is superior or of more value than the other.

Consider also the original divine establishment of marriage:

Therefore a man shall leave his father and his mother and hold fast to his wife, and they shall become one flesh. (Genesis 2:24)

Here we see that man and woman enter into an exclusive and intimate partnership (one flesh) to serve as God's image-bearers. While the man and woman are distinct, they share the same substance. As

---

8   See John Walton, *The NIV Application Commentary: Genesis* (Grand Rapids, MI: Zondervan, 2001): "To conclude, then, (1) since there are a couple of contexts in which *šmr* ["take care of"] is used for Levitical service along with *ʿbd* ["work"] (e.g., Num. 3:8–9), (2) since the contextual use of *šmr* here favors sacred service, (3) since *ʿbd* is as likely to refer to sacred service as to agricultural tasks, and (4) since there are other indications that the garden is being portrayed as sacred space, it is likely that the tasks given to Adam are of a priestly nature—that is, caring for sacred space." (p. 173)

9   J.K. McKee, *Men and Women in the Body of Messiah: Answering Crucial Questions* (Richardson, TX: Messianic Apologetics, 2018), p. 10

John Walton puts it, "Woman is recognized as being of the same essence as man and therefore of serving as his ally in sacred space."[10] Moreover, man is said to leave (literally forsake) his previous family commitments. This teaches us that a man's first loyalty is not to his parents or tribe but to his wife. He "holds fast" to her, which is a phrase often used to express the covenant commitment one is to have toward God (e.g., Deuteronomy 10:20; 30:20).

Marriage is a bond wherein the wife is honored, cherished, and protected by her husband. The sexual union is to be enjoyed only within the boundaries of this covenant relationship between man and wife. Thus, according to Genesis, women aren't inferior beings or property that can be used and abused by men. No, they are equal partners with men in the divine purpose to glorify God on earth.

These passages establish a "creation ideal," which represents God's ideal model for humanity before sin. This model teaches male-female equality and partnership in God's creation and plan. Though men and women are distinct, they share the same essence. Both are made in God's image, and therefore both are endowed with intrinsic worth and elected to serve God's purposes. Men and women need each other; both genders have something unique to offer that the other lacks. Men are hindered in their ability to serve as God's image-bearers without women, and women are hindered without men.[11]

---

10   John Walton, *NIV Cultural Backgrounds Study Bible: Bringing to Life the Ancient World of Scripture* (Grand Rapids, MI: Zondervan, 2016), p. 11

11   This is not to say that an unmarried person cannot serve God fully or properly because they aren't partnered with a person of the other gender in marriage. Marriage is *one* expression of male-female partnership in service to God. Another expression of men and women working together in service to God is the Church, made up of both male and female members who utilize their God-given gifts to further God's kingdom.

Passages Allegedly Indicating Female Inferiority in the Garden

While some feminists might agree with the conclusions established so far, others object to the idea that God's creation ideal establishes male-female equality. Some take a more cynical view, highlighting certain features of the narrative such as the fact that woman is created *after* man and formed *out of* him. These features, it is said, indicate that woman has an inferior status—she is an afterthought who is dependent upon man for life and created solely to fix his loneliness and to be ruled over by him. However, as George W. Ramsey helpfully points out, "The later creation of woman no more signifies inferiority to man than the creation of humans subsequent to the lower animals in Genesis 1 signifies human inferiority; the derivation of woman 'out of' man cannot be taken as a sign of her inferiority any more than can man's being made 'out of' the ground be taken as a sign of man's inferiority to the ground."[12] The only way to derive the idea of female inferiority from such biblical statements is to approach the text wanting desperately to find it. Such a view is read *into* the text, not naturally gleaned from the text.

Often Genesis 2:18 is cited to support the idea that the Bible regards women as inferior beings made only to serve men:

> Then the Lord God said, "It is not good that the man should be alone; I will make him a helper fit for him." (Genesis 2:18)

It's argued that the creation of woman to be man's "helper" implies female inferiority or subordination. However, when we look at the

---

12 George W. Ramsey, "Is Name-Giving an Act of Domination in Genesis 2:23 and elsewhere?" *CBQ*, Vol. 50, No. 1 (1988), p. 24 (n. 3)

Hebrew word for "helper" (*ezer*) in this verse, we find that this word in itself does not suggest an inferior status at all. For instance, most of the occurrences of the word refer to God Himself as the "helper" of His people (e.g., Psalm 33:20; 115:9; 121:1-2). Obviously, God is not inferior to His people—He's superior!—and yet the authors of Scripture say that God is our helper. Other times, the word refers to the military "help" of other nations (Isaiah 30:5; Ezekiel 12:14). As we can see, while ezer is "a relational term, describing a beneficial relationship," the word itself "does not specify position or rank, either superiority or inferiority."[13]

What, then, does this verse teach us about the status of women? The immediate context brings some clarity: God said He will make a helper "fit" for man. This word is *kenegdo*, which literally translates to "like his counterpart, corresponding to him."[14] This suggests equality, not inferiority. The woman being a "fit/suitable helper" for the man can therefore be better understood as "ideal partner."[15] God identifies a problem: man is alone. There is no fit companion for man among the animals. Thus, God creates an ideal partner to "help" man's aloneness so that humans can effectively serve God's

---

13   Richard M. Davidson, "Headship, Submission, and Equality in Scripture" in *Women in Ministry: Biblical and Historical Perspectives.* Nancy Vyhmeister, ed. (Berrien Springs, MI: Andrews University Press, 1998), p. 262

14   Ibid.

15   See Linda Belleville, "Women in Ministry: An Egalitarian Perspective," *Two Views on Women in Ministry.* James R. Beck, ed. (Grand Rapids, MI: Zondervan, 2005): "The woman was created as a help 'in correspondence to' (kenegdo) the man. This, once again, is the language of sameness, not superiority. The 'she' is the personal counterpart in every way to the 'he.' Therefore, 'partner' (REB, NAB, NRSV, CEV)—and not 'helper'— accurately captures the sense of the Hebrew term *ezer.*" (p. 28)

purposes together. As Alice Matthews puts it, "Eve was not created to serve Adam but serve *with* him."[16]

Thus, the assertion that Genesis 2:18 prescribes female inferiority is wrong. There is no implicit notion of inferiority embedded in the term *ezer*, "helper." Again, such an idea is read *into* the text rather than read naturally from the text.

Genesis 2:23 is another verse that is sometimes cited to demonstrate the alleged sexism of the Bible:

> Then the man said, "This at last is bone of my bones and flesh of my flesh; she shall be called Woman, because she was taken out of Man." (Genesis 2:23)

Critics complain that the man "names" woman like he named the animals, which would be an act of domination over her. However, according to John Walton, such a reading of Genesis 2:23 would be a mistake.[17] Walton points out that when Adam named the animals in Genesis 2:19-20, a different vocabulary and syntax are used. In Genesis 2:23, Adam was not naming the woman but merely indicating that she belongs to the category of humankind. This interpretation is confirmed when we consider that man refers to the woman as "bone of my bones and flesh of my flesh" in the same verse, which certainly isn't a statement one would expect if the text was intended to teach that woman is inferior to man.

One more passage deserves our attention:

---

16 Alice Mathews, *Gender Roles and the People of God: Rethinking What We Were Taught about Men and Women in the Church* (Grand Rapids: Zondervan, 2017), p. 39

17 John Walton, *The NIV Application Commentary: Genesis* (Grand Rapids, MI: Zondervan, 2001), p. 178

> So when the woman saw that the tree was good for food, and
> that it was a delight to the eyes, and that the tree was to be
> desired to make one wise, she took of its fruit and ate, and she
> also gave some to her husband who was with her, and he ate.
> (Genesis 3:6)

The woman listened to the voice of the serpent and ate from the tree of knowledge of good and evil in violation of God's commandment. She then gave some of the fruit to her husband, who also ate. Based on this, feminists will claim that the Bible vilifies the woman (who is a symbol for *all* women) as being responsible for all the sin and death in the world.[18] However, when we read the text without a preconceived bias, we discover that the blame cannot be placed at the feet of the woman alone.[19] Why? Because Adam was with her the whole time: "…and she also gave some to her husband *who was with her*" (Genesis 3:6). In further support of this fact, Walton points out that all the Hebrew verbs in the section are plural: "From verse 1 where the serpent addressed the woman but uses the plural 'you,' to the woman's use of inclusionary 'we' and the serpent's description of the results formulated to both, there is every grammatical indication that both are there."[20] Both the man and the

---

18 See Lauri Weissman, "Half Human: How Jewish Law Justifies the Exclusion and Exploitation of Women," *Women v. Religion: The Case Against Faith—and for Freedom.* Karen L. Garst, ed. (Durham, NC: Pitchstone Publishing, 2018): "Original sin explicitly indicts women, and our desire for knowledge above our station, as the literal root of all evil." (pp. 50-51)

19 See Chapter 7 for an explanation of 1 Timothy 2:11-15.

20 John Walton, *The NIV Application Commentary: Genesis* (Grand Rapids, MI: Zondervan, 2001), p. 206

woman are therefore responsible for bringing sin and death into the world.

After Eden

As I mentioned previously, Genesis 1-2 establishes God's "creation ideal" for humans, which fully affirms equality between men and women. However, after the fall, this relationship was cursed:

> To the woman He said, "I will greatly multiply Your pain in childbirth, In pain you will bring forth children; Yet **your desire will be for your husband, And he will rule over you.**" (Genesis 3:16, NASB, emphasis added)

Adam and Eve's sin brought about conflict in the relationship between men and women: she will possess a "desire" for her husband, and he will "rule over" her. The woman's desire (*teshuqah*) suggests an urge to dominate her husband. The only other place this word occurs in Genesis is when God warns Cain that sin is crouching at the door ready to pounce—its "desire" is for Cain, and he must rule over it (Genesis 4:7). As Victor P. Hamilton writes:

> [T]he desire of the woman for her husband is akin to the desire of sin that lies poised ready to leap at Cain. It means a desire to break the relationship of equality and turn it into a relationship of servitude and domination. The sinful husband will try to be a tyrant over his wife. Far from being a reign of co-equals over the remainder of God's creation, the relationship now becomes a fierce dispute, with each party trying to

rule the other. The two who reigned as one attempt to rule each other.[21]

Contrary to popular belief, Genesis 3:16 is not God assigning gender roles but instead describing the inevitable consequences of sin. Rather than being inclined toward unity and partnership, man and woman will be in conflict. The woman will try to dominate her man, and the man, who is physically stronger than the woman, "will have no choice but to overpower her in such a situation."[22] Man's total power over women certainly describes the ancient Near Eastern culture in which the Bible was written—but this state of affairs is not God's original will for His creation!

Again, the creation ideal is male-female equality and partnership, as we see in Genesis 1-2. After the fall, God lovingly condescends to deal with humans in their fallen state while pointing them back toward the creation model as much as possible. One of the ways He does this is by giving mankind the Torah, which "lays the first stepping stones back to the male and female equality, and shared responsibility, as originally experienced in Eden."[23]

Since the Torah is given within the parameters of post-fall ancient Near Eastern society, we'll see examples of God working within man-made societal structures (e.g., slavery). But we understand that God does not necessarily endorse the structures themselves. In the midst of imperfect systems that existed due to the nature of our fallen world, God provides regulations that protected the vulnerable who were often

---

21   Victor P. Hamilton, *New International Commentary on the Old Testament: The Book of Genesis, Chapters 1-17* (Grand Rapids: Eerdmans, 1990), p. 202, quoted in J.K. McKee, *Messianic Torah Helper* (McKinney, TX: Messianic Apologetics, 2016)

22   J.K. McKee, *Messianic Torah Helper* (McKinney, TX: Messianic Apologetics, 2016), p. 38

23   Ibid.

abused within such systems. By doing this, the Bible emphasizes the personhood and equality of all people, setting a trajectory back to the creation ideal.

Yeshua taught this principle when He said of the laws permitting divorce, "from the beginning it was not so" (Matthew 19:8). Divorce is not the creation ideal but a concession to human frailty.[24] It's a consequence of sin and, sadly, a reality of our fallen world. Thus, God's laws regulating (but not endorsing) situations like divorce highlighted the dignity of the people involved and established barriers to prevent mistreatment.[25]

In the midst of our fallen world, God is calling us back to creation. That is the intended model for humanity. But God's approach to reaching that goal with respect to ancient Israel was to meet them where they were and *gradually* lead them toward a better way. Rather than

---

24 See C.E.B. Cranfield, *The Bible and Christian Life* (T & T Clark, 1985): "Jesus, by referring to the hardness of heart which necessitated the provision, by reminding His questioners of the Genesis account of God's original institution of marriage (vv. 6–8), and by His clear prohibition, 'What therefore God hath joined together, let not man put asunder' (v. 9), was not (as is often alleged) brushing aside Deut 24:1 and taking a rigorist stance, but was drawing attention to something extremely important which the Pharisees were inclined to ignore, namely, the need to distinguish clearly between those elements of the OT law which set forth the perfect will of God (what we may call—in one sense of the word—His absolute will, that is, His will in itself, not affected by the fact and the results of human sin), on the one hand, and, on the other hand, those elements which, taking into account the fact of men's sinfulness, indicate not God's perfect, absolute will, but His will in response to the circumstances brought about by human sin." (pp. 229-230)

25 See Paul Copan, *Is God a Moral Monster?: Making Sense of the Old Testament God* (Grand Rapids, MI: Baker Publishing Group, 2011): "The certificate of divorce was to protect the wife; a vulnerable divorced woman typically had to remarry to escape poverty and shame by coming under the shelter of a husband. This law took into consideration the well-being of the wife so that she wouldn't be divorced and taken back and then dumped once more at the whim of her former husband." (p. 64)

prohibiting societal systems like slavery outright, which probably wouldn't have been effective considering how deeply engrained such structures were in the ancient world,[26] God permitted them and regulated them on the basis of human value and equality. His laws that are given within the framework of such systems constantly remind us that all men and women are our neighbors and thus worthy of dignity and honor like we are: "You shall love your neighbor *as yourself*" (Leviticus 19:18).

That said, throughout the Bible, a patriarchal system in which the father held legal authority and responsibility for the household, is assumed. The father's leadership and authority, as Davidson explains, "are evidenced in such concerns as family inheritance and ownership of property, contracting marriages for the children, and overall responsibility in speaking for his family."[27] In other words, within the culture in which the Bible was written, a husband/father was the primary legal and religious representative of the family. Patriarchy can simply be defined as a societal system in which men hold primary power and leadership roles.

Feminists complain that religious patriarchy "perpetuates and protects the systemic abuse of women, both in institutions and in

---

26 See Alden Thompson, *Who's Afraid of the Old Testament God?* (Energion Publications, 1989): "Judged by the cultures around ancient Israel, the laws given to Israel show remarkable signs of 'humanization.' God took this people, in spite of the many barbaric and cruel customs which they had adopted, and began to draw them to him. He wished to show them a better way. But if human beings are to be treated as real human beings who possess the power of choice, then the 'better way' must come gradually. Otherwise, they will exercise their freedom of choice and turn away from that which they do not understand." (Kindle Locations 429-433)

27 Richard M. Davidson, *Flame of Yahweh: Sexuality in the Old Testament* (Peabody, MA: Hendrickson Publishers, 2007), p. 215

religiously influenced families and marriages."[28] But is this complaint valid? How should we think about the Bible's incorporation of patriarchal structures?

First, we remember that "from the beginning it was not so." Man-made societal systems like patriarchy are not God's creation ideal for humanity. The Bible does not demand that we reinstall a patriarchal society. Certainly the values and principles expressed in God's word transcend culture and still apply to us today (e.g. honor and protection within the family), but the cultural form in which these laws were originally given does not need to be recreated.

This leads to my second point: the intention of the Torah is not to unequivocally endorse these man-made societal systems. Rather, the laws of Moses "work within the patriarchal framework and regulate this system, providing a degree of care and protection for women and children."[29] God's laws governing Israel's patriarchal society included measures that prevented the oppression and abuse of women, as we will see throughout this book. Theologian Katie McCoy sums it up nicely: "Old Testament law restrained powerful men and defended vulnerable women."[30] This value of protecting the vulnerable is the goal of many of God's commands in the Torah, and it remains a moral imperative for the Church today.

In addition to biblical patriarchy being regulated to protect women, another point worth mentioning is that women in the

---

28 Lauri Weissman, "Half Human: How Jewish Law Justifies the Exclusion and Exploitation of Women," *Women v. Religion: The Case Against Faith—and for Freedom.* Karen L. Garst, ed. (Durham, NC: Pitchstone Publishing, 2018), p. 72

29 Richard M. Davidson, *Flame of Yahweh: Sexuality in the Old Testament* (Peabody, MA: Hendrickson Publishers, 2007), p. 218

30 Katie McCoy, *Credo.* "The Old Testament Law and Women." www.credomag.com. Accessed 12/8/19

ancient world didn't consider *biblical* patriarchy to be oppressive. While our modern society values individualism and self-fulfillment above all else, the ancient world in which the Bible was written was a collectivist culture, "which values one's responsibility to and harmony within the community, especially the family."[31] A woman in the ancient world would have welcomed the supervision and protection of her husband/father in legal and religious matters. Modern feminists make a mistake when they arrogantly impose their own feelings and cultural biases onto ancient women.

Finally, while the husband/father did function as the leader of the household in the Bible, according to Daniel Block, "the OT pays relatively little attention to the power of the husband and father."[32] Block further explains that this emphasis on "the responsibilities associated with headship over the household (as opposed to its privileges and power) is consistent with the overall tenor of the OT, which views leadership in general to be a privilege granted to an individual in order to serve the interests of those who were led."[33] Thus, the biblical portrayal of the husband's/father's leadership in the family is not one of domination and power over women but of loving responsibility for those in his care. He is the servant-leader of the family to whom the wife voluntarily and lovingly submits.

Nevertheless, even within the patriarchal framework permitted throughout the Bible, there are "undeniable affirmations of equality in the Old Testament from theological, historical, and legal perspectives."[34] What are some clear examples of male-female equality in the

31 Ibid.

32 Daniel Block, "You Shall Not Covet Your Neighbor's Wife: A Study in Deuteronomic Domestic Ideology," *Journal of the Evangelical Theological Society*, Vol. 53 (2010), p. 451

33 Ibid., p. 452

34 Paul Copan, *Is God a Moral Monster?: Making Sense of the Old Testament God* (Grand

Bible after Eden? Well, we find hints of the creation ideal embedded all over the biblical text. For example, consider the Fifth Commandment:

> Honor your **father and your mother**, that your days may be long in the land that the Lord your God is giving you. (Exodus 20:12, emphasis added)

Many of us who have grown up in the Church have heard this commandment so many times that we tend to gloss over it. But if we stop to read it, we can see that the Bible, once again, is clearly affirming the equality of man and woman. Father *and* mother are equally worthy of honor within the family. This biblical value is in stark contrast to the values of other cultures in the ancient Near East, where the mother was actually controlled by her son. Davidson speaks to the significance of these biblical commands:

> According to the fifth commandment of the Decalogue and repeated commands throughout the pentateuchal codes, the wife/mother was to be given equal honor to the father within the family circle (Exod 20:12; 21:15,17; Lev 20:9; Deut 21:18-21; 27:16). There is no discrimination in favor of father and against mother. The mother's authority over the son is as great in the law codes as is that of the father. The same penalty is imposed upon the son for striking or cursing his father or his mother (Exod 21: 15, 17). In fact, within a Near Eastern milieu in which the mother was often controlled by the son, Lev 19:3 surprisingly places the mother first instead of the father in the command: "You shall each revere your mother and

---

Rapids, MI: Baker Publishing Group, 2011), p. 103

father." This reversal from normal order clearly emphasizes the woman's right to equal filial respect along with her husband.[35]

Additionally, the Torah expresses the equality of men and women in regard to morality, purity, and justice. As Paul Copan observes, "The moral and ceremonial laws of Israel presumed that women were not only equal but also shared equal moral responsibility with the men."[36] As full members of God's covenant family (Deuteronomy 29:9-12), women, along with men, are fully accountable to God and expected to learn and do the Torah (Deuteronomy 31:12). Women also receive the same benefits as men in the Torah (e.g., a weekly Sabbath, Exodus 20:8-10). Women who violate certain commands in the Torah, such as the laws against adultery, are subject to the same punishment as men (Leviticus 20:10). God's law is absolute, unlike other ancient Near Eastern law codes, which seem to have a more "subjective and variable approach."[37] The reason is that the authors of these other law codes saw married women as the property of their husbands, unlike the

---

35   Richard M. Davidson, *Flame of Yahweh: Sexuality in the Old Testament* (Peabody, MA: Hendrickson Publishers, 2007), p. 250

36   Paul Copan, *Is God a Moral Monster?: Making Sense of the Old Testament God* (Grand Rapids, MI: Baker Publishing Group, 2011), p. 104

37   See John Walton, "Penalties for Sexual Offenses in Biblical and Mesopotamian Law," *NIV Cultural Backgrounds Study Bible: Bringing to Life the Ancient World of Scripture* (Grand Rapids, MI: Zondervan, 2016): "Mesopotamian law treated premeditated adultery as a crime punishable by death, as in Biblical law. However, the Mesopotamians had a more subjective and variable approach to other kinds of cases. There were distinctions between degrees of adultery, depending on degrees of intention, with circumstances affecting the severity of penalties. An adulteress who had not premeditated the act was under her husband's jurisdiction, and whatever punishment he decided for her was also meted out to her paramour." (p. 216).

Torah, which treated crimes like adultery as "primarily a moral crime against God and not merely a personal injury to the husband."[38]

When you get to the New Testament, the creation ideal of male-female equality is fully reaffirmed. All who have exercised faith in Yeshua—whether Jew or Greek, slave or free, *male or female*—stand equal before the Father in regard to being justified and included among His people (Galatians 3:28). Women are joint heirs "of the grace of life" (1 Peter 3:7). Nowhere does the Bible teach that women have a lesser position than men in Messiah's Kingdom.

In contrast to the low view of women expressed in the Greco-Roman culture surrounding the early church, followers of Messiah promoted equality and protection for women by prohibiting unwarranted divorce, prostitution, polygamy, homosexual behavior, and marital infidelity. In the Greco-Roman society of Paul's day, women were expected to be faithful to their husbands while the men had virtually no moral limits on their sexual conduct. Married men often engaged in extra-marital affairs with "girlfriends, mistresses, prostitutes, courtesans, other men, and, most of all, household slaves," forcing their wives to have to "compete with a host of other people for their husband's love and attention."[39] In opposition to this cultural double-standard, Paul taught that infidelity on the part of the husband is no less severe a sin than infidelity on the part of the wife, demonstrating once again the creation ideal of equality. Paul instructed husbands not to pursue extra-marital sex with slaves and prostitutes, but that "a man's erotic desire, affection, and sexual energy

---

38 Richard M. Davidson, *Flame of Yahweh: Sexuality in the Old Testament* (Peabody, MA: Hendrickson Publishers, 2007), p. 250

39 Nancy R. Pearcey, *Love Thy Body: Answering Hard Questions about Life and Sexuality* (Grand Rapids, MI: Baker Books, 2018), p. 186

should be focused on his wife."[40] According to the Bible, a husband not only has authority over his wife's body but *a wife* has authority over *her husband's* body (1 Corinthians 7:3-4).

Christianity's sexual ethic and opposition to the practices of abortion and infanticide were among many reasons women in the ancient world were so drawn to the early church.[41] Christianity was also responsible for passing the first laws against sexual slavery, elevating the status of countless oppressed and exploited women in the ancient world.[42] In fact, as Michael Kruger points out, Christianity was so popular among women that its earliest pagan critics, such as the philosopher Celsus, mocked it as being a "religion of women."[43]

Christianity not only elevated the status of women but also provided women meaningful involvement in Christian ministry. Paul recognized that women were not prohibited from praying and prophesying in the church (1 Corinthians 11:5). The book of Acts declared that both Spirit-filled men and women are called to prophesy in accordance with biblical prophecy (Acts 2:17-18;

---

40   Ibid., p. 146

41   Ibid., esp. Chapter 2

42   Kyle Harper, *From Shame to Sin: The Christian Transformation of Sexual Morality in Late Antiquity* (Cambridge, MA: Harvard University Press, 2013): "In AD 428 the Christian emperor Theodosius II enacted a law banning the use of coercion in the sex industry. The law wished to repress the prostitution of slaves, daughters, and other vulnerable members of society, which was anything but a marginal part of the classical sexual order. The moral foundations of the law were, there can be no doubt, Christian [...] The complete, violent exploitation of women without any claim to civic protection was simply, as a problem in its own right, invisible in a culture whose moral foundations were immanent in the logic of social reproduction. The law of 428 was the first salvo in an enduring crusade against coercive procurement that the Christian emperors of the next century would carry out." (p. 8)

43   Michael Kruger, *Canon Fodder*. "Was Early Christianity Hostile to Women?" www.michaeljkruger.com. Accessed 10/22/19

Joel 2:28-29). Women also participated in apostolic and teaching ministry (Acts 18:26; Romans 16:3, 7; Philippians 4:2-3). Again, men and women were both created in God's image and thus given intrinsic value *and purpose*. This message is consistent throughout the Bible from the beginning.

Finally, Yeshua, the eternal Son of God Himself, expressed the value and equality of women in the eyes of God through the way He treated them and interacted with them. In the face of cultural and religious pressures, Yeshua ministered to the Samaritan woman at the well. He even entered into a lengthy theological discussion with her, honoring her desire to worship God in truth (John 4:1-45). Even though a woman's testimony was generally regarded as untrustworthy in this time and culture,[44] the Bible elevated women in spite of these cultural sentiments by intentionally mentioning that the Samaritan woman's testimony was unhesitatingly received by her community (John 4:39).

Yeshua even allowed women to be His disciples and respected their desire to learn from Him. In opposition to the cultural expectations of His day, Yeshua praised Mary for sitting at His feet and listening to His teachings alongside His male disciples (Luke 10:42). This is not a trivial point to be overlooked! As New Testament scholar N.T. Wright explains, "[T]o sit at the teacher's feet is a way of saying you are being a *student* and picking up the teacher's wisdom and learning; in that very practical world, you wouldn't do this just for the sake of informing your own mind and heart, but in order to become

---

44   See Josephus, *Antiquities* 4.8.15 (translated by William Whiston): "But let not the testimony of women be admitted, on account of the levity and boldness of their sex [...] since it is probable that they may not speak truth."

yourself a teacher, a rabbi."[45] Yeshua further expressed God's mercy and compassion toward women by healing and delivering them (Luke 8:2, 43-48; 13:12). In His teachings on divorce, Yeshua elevated the status of women by prohibiting men from divorcing them for "any cause"[46] (Matthew 19:3-9).

When you take an overall look at the treatment of women in the Bible, their dignity and value expressed therein are evident. You cannot deny God's utmost concern for their protection and wellbeing. The very definition of pure and undefiled religion, according to the Bible, is to care for vulnerable women and children (James 1:27). Their mistreatment is strictly forbidden, and God Himself promises to execute His wrath upon anyone who harms them (Exodus 22:22). Indeed, one of God's titles is the "protector of widows" (Psalm 68:5). Not only that, but the fact that women, like men, are treated as being fully accountable to God is decidedly clear. Women are equal members of God's covenant family, with the same responsibility and mission as that of men—to glorify God and serve as His image-bearers. That is not to say that the Bible doesn't contain some difficult passages that appear to treat women as property or inferior to men (we will explore those in later chapters of this book), but perhaps those passages and topics can now be better understood in light of what we've established so far.

---

45 N.T. Wright, *Surprised by Scripture: Engaging Contemporary Issues* (New York, NY: HarperCollins Publishers, 2014), p. 70

46 One of reasons given for divorce at this time included the wife ruining her husband's dinner. Later rabbis ruled that divorce was allowed if the man simply found someone they thought was more physically attractive (m.Gittin 9.10).

Women in the Bible

Before we move on to address specific challenges from feminists, atheists, and others who are critical of the Bible, let's look at how the Scriptures portray various women. If the Bible were genuinely misogynistic, we would expect that it would never honor women or highlight their courage, faith, wisdom, and other positive attributes. We would expect never to find women functioning and succeeding in positions of influence and leadership. We would expect never to see women playing a central role in God's unfolding story. And yet, a survey of the Scriptures dismantles those expectations,[47] which would entail that perhaps the idea that the Bible is misogynistic should be revisited.

Consider the matriarch Sarah. Feminists have complained that Sarah has been "left out" of the story "as if she didn't exist."[48] While many might assume that God's covenant promises to bring forth the nation of Israel and bless the nations of the earth involved only Abraham, Sarah is revealed to have been just as essential to God's plan as her husband. Indeed, the Bible not only emphasizes Abraham's seed but also makes clear that it is *Sarah's* seed that will fulfill the promise (Genesis 17:18-19; 21:12). The prophet Isaiah tells Israel to "look to Abraham your father *and* to Sarah who bore you" (Isaiah 51:2), highlighting once again Sarah's critical role as the matriarch of Israel.

---

47   I would like to express my gratitude for the work of Jo Ann Davidson and Richard M. Davidson, which has been very helpful to me in putting together the material in this section. See Jo Ann Davidson, "Women in Scripture: A Survey and Evaluation," *Women in Ministry: Biblical and Historical Perspectives.* Nancy Vyhmeister, ed. (Berrien Springs, MI: Andrews University Press, 1998), pp. 157-179; Richard M. Davidson, *Flame of Yahweh: Sexuality in the Old Testament* (Peabody, MA: Hendrickson Publishers, 2007), pp. 226-240

48   Karen Garst, *Faithless Feminist.* "What Happened to Sarah?" www.faithlessfeminist.com. Accessed 9/16/19

Hagar was a rejected slave woman to man, but a closer look at her narrative reveals her to be a highly honored and loved woman to God. The "Angel of the Lord" made his first appearance in the biblical story to none other than Hagar, even addressing her by name (Genesis 16:8). When Abraham and Sarah banished Hagar, God visited her and provided for her and her son. He promised her that He would make a great nation from her son, which is identical to the promise He made to Abraham in regard to Isaac (Genesis 16:10; 21:18). Jo Ann Davidson observes that this is "the only time that a covenantal-type promise was announced to a woman."[49]

The matriarch Rebekah is far from being a mere "extra" in God's story. Like Abraham, she is praised in the Scriptures for her faith and hospitality. Scripture presents her as playing a central part in God's plan. In addition to being beautiful (Genesis 24:16), Rebekah is portrayed as faithful and strong. Feminists often allege that biblical women were treated as property and had no say regarding whom they could marry. But when Abraham commissions Eleazar to find a wife for his son Isaac, he says, "If the woman is not willing to follow you, then you will be free from this oath of mine" (Genesis 24:8). He leaves it up the woman to decide whether or not she will go with Eleazar. And that's precisely what we see—Rebekah herself made the decision to marry Isaac (Genesis 24:58). What's perhaps most astonishing about Rebekah are the intentional parallels between her and Abraham on the part of the biblical author. As Dr. Tikva Frymer-Kensky writes:

---

49   Jo Ann Davidson, "Women in Scripture: A Survey and Evaluation," *Women in Ministry: Biblical and Historical Perspectives.* Nancy Vyhmeister, ed. (Berrien Springs, MI: Andrews University Press, 1998), p. 163

Rivka is the counterpart to both Abraham and Sarah. Like
Sarah, she is the instrument of the promise, the agent through
whom Isaac will become the father of a nation. She is also a
second Abraham, who, like him, voluntarily chooses to leave
Mesopotamia for Canaan. Her "I will go" answers the four
times the issue of going has been raised in the story (vv. 4, 7,
38, and 40) and echoes God's command to Abraham to "Go!"
in Gen. 12:1 [...] Rivka is very much like Abraham. They are
both models of hospitality, and the narrator of her story highlights her similarity to him by describing her actions toward
the emissary in the same language that describes Abraham's
actions toward his angel visitors (Gen. 18:1-8).[50]

Rachel and Leah are also shown to be tremendous women of
courage and strength. In Genesis 31, we see that they stood up to their
father, who tried to withhold their inheritance from them. And like
Abraham, they were willing to leave their homeland and go where God
called them.

In regard to the Genesis Matriarchs, Davidson insightfully concludes:

The Genesis matriarchs are not wallflowers. They are not little
housewives; they are the founders of the nation. It would
be unfair to the portraits of these women to argue that the
Genesis matriarchs bow in submission to all men or are under
the oppressive authority of their husbands. Rather, though
respectful of their husbands, they are intelligent, forceful, and

---

50   Tikva Frymer-Kensky, *Reading the Women of the Bible: A New Interpretation of Their
Stories* (New York: Schocken Books, 2002), pp. 13-14

directive [...] Feminists are right in demanding redress of the long-accumulating record of the subjugation of women. But they need to rethink the cause of this repression. The Genesis matriarchs were not suppressed or oppressed women.[51]

Beyond Genesis, we could cite many more examples of highly valued and influential women. Shiphrah and Puah, for instance, are highlighted in the Scriptures as the two midwives who saved countless lives by courageously defying an evil decree by the Pharaoh of Egypt (Exodus 1:15-21). Because of their bravery, God blessed them (Exodus 1:20-21). As Trevor Dennis writes, "Of all the initiatives taken by human beings in Ex 1-14, it is those of the women, however, that display the greatest courage, invite our keenest admiration, and have the most powerful influence on events."[52]

Miriam, the sister of Moses and Aaron, is identified as a leader and prophetess (Exodus 15:20). The Bible highlights her "intelligence, diplomacy, and courage to speak to the Egyptian princess, cleverly suggesting a 'nurse' for the baby in the basket."[53] The prophet Micah specifically cites Miriam, along with Moses and Aaron, as leading Israel out of Egypt: "For I brought you up from the land of

---

51   Richard M. Davidson, *Flame of Yahweh: Sexuality in the Old Testament* (Peabody, MA: Hendrickson Publishers, 2007), pp. 235

52   Trevor Dennis, *Sarah Laughed: Women's Voices in the Old Testament* (Nashville: Abingdon, 1994), p.114, quoted in Jo Ann Davidson, "Women in Scripture: A Survey and Evaluation," *Women in Ministry: Biblical and Historical Perspectives*. Nancy Vyhmeister, ed. (Berrien Springs, MI: Andrews University Press, 1998)

53   Jo Ann Davidson, "Women in Scripture: A Survey and Evaluation," *Women in Ministry: Biblical and Historical Perspectives*. Nancy Vyhmeister, ed. (Berrien Springs, MI: Andrews University Press, 1998), p. 166

Egypt and redeemed you from the house of slavery, and I sent before you Moses, Aaron, and Miriam" (Micah 6:4).

Rahab is presented in Scripture as displaying faith, courage, and hospitality, for which she's honored by the apostles (James 2:25; Hebrews 11:31). Deborah is praised as a prominent judge, prophetess, and military leader of Israel (Judges 4-5). Ruth is portrayed as a woman of tremendous faith who, like Abraham, left everything behind to serve God; she is recognized as "a vital link in the covenantal history between God and his people, not only with the Davidic king, but as an ancestor of the Messiah."[54] Huldah was a prophetess and the head advisor to King Josiah (2 Kings 22:14-20; 2 Chronicles 34:22-28). The book of Esther highlights the courage of a young Jewish woman whose God-ordained position of influence (Esther 4:14) allowed her to bravely petition the king of Persia on behalf of her people, saving them from destruction. The author of Proverbs 31 paints a portrait of an "excellent" woman who is praised not for her physical beauty but for her wisdom, kindness, strength, trustworthiness, intelligence, generosity, and for being hardworking.

In the New Testament, several women are identified as prophetesses: Anna (Luke 2:36) and Philip's four daughters (Acts 21:9). Junia is described as an apostle (Romans 16:7). Priscilla is described as a missionary (Acts 18; Romans 16:3). Priscilla, along with her husband, even tutored the great Messianic Jewish apologist, Apollos (Acts 18:26). Paul acknowledges Euodia and Synthyche as fellow laborers in the Gospel, serving alongside Paul himself (Philippians 4:2-3). Phoebe, the courier of Paul's epistle to the community of believers in Rome, is identified as a "deacon" of the church at Cenchreae (Romans 16:1). This title is the same Greek term (*diakonos*) that Paul uses for ministry

---

54   Ibid., p. 168

leaders elsewhere in his letters (e.g., 1 Timothy 3:8-10). As Tim Hegg suggests, "There is every reason to believe, therefore, that Phoebe held an official position in the congregation at Cenchreae, and that she did so without regard to her gender."[55]

Perhaps most significant, however, is the account of Yeshua's resurrection—the very basis of our faith. Paul said, "If Christ has not been raised, your faith is futile" (1 Corinthians 15:17). And yet, in God's sovereign wisdom and plan, the first ones to discover Yeshua's empty tomb and to meet the risen Lord were His women followers. Yeshua told them to inform his brothers, enlisting these women as the very first evangelists to testify of His resurrection (Matthew 28:1-10). Think about that. The first people to be entrusted with declaring the Messiah's resurrection from the dead were women!

When we examine the matter carefully and in context, the Scriptures—both Old and New Testaments—clearly affirm the immense value of women. Along with men, women are created in the image of God and endowed with intrinsic worth and purpose. Even after the fall, the Bible continually points us back toward this creation ideal; God builds much of the Torah on the basis of human dignity and equality, providing care and protection for women. Many women, like many men, are praised for their faith, courage, strength, and wisdom throughout the biblical narrative. They are described as leaders, prophetesses, and as playing crucial roles in God's unfolding story.

In conclusion, no, God is not a misogynist. If you are still struggling with concerns about the Bible's treatment of women, the following chapters will address common objections based on specific passages. Hopefully the rest of this book will help to clarify these important issues and reinforce the conclusion reached in this chapter.

---

55   Tim Hegg, *Paul's Epistle to the Romans* (Tacoma, WA: TorahResource, 2007), p. 447

CHAPTER 2
DOES GOD ENDORSE POLYGAMY?

One of the reasons given in support of the claim that God views women as "property" and inferior to men is the Bible's alleged endorsement of polygamy—that is, the practice whereby a man is married to more than one woman at the same time.[1] Why Does the Bible regard men like King David and Abraham—men who practiced polygamy—with such high esteem? Should the Bible's regulations of this practice (e.g., Deuteronomy 21:15-17) be considered a sign of endorsement? Where do we begin to understand this issue?

The Messiah's teaching on divorce, which touches on this issue, is a good starting point. When Yeshua was asked about divorce in Matthew 19, His response was not to quibble with the Pharisees over the nuances of particular laws in the Torah governing divorce. Now, He didn't disregard parts of the Torah or consider them irrelevant by any means; He affirmed the ongoing validity and authority of every "iota" and "dot" of the Torah (e.g., Matthew 5:17-20). However, Yeshua recognized that divorce was not representative of the creation ideal. As theologian Charles Cranfield notes, He "was not (as is often alleged) brushing aside Deut 24:1" but rather drawing attention to "the need to distinguish clearly between those elements of the OT law which set forth the perfect will of God" and "those elements which, taking

---

1   Technically, the practice whereby a man has multiple wives at the same time is a specific type of polygamy called polygyny. Polygamy is the practice of having more than one spouse at the same time and can refer to a man having multiple wives as well as to a woman having multiple husbands. For the sake of simplicity, I will use the more familiar term, polygamy.

into account the fact of men's sinfulness, indicate not God's perfect, absolute will, but His will in response to the circumstances brought about by human sin."[2] In either case, Yeshua's answer centered not on what established legitimate warrant for divorce but on God's intention for marriage in the beginning—that a man and a woman become one: "So they are no longer two but one flesh" (Matthew 19:6). The original marriage in creation establishes the model for all marriages from Yeshua's perspective. God brings the husband and wife together; therefore, "what God has joined together, let not man separate" (Matthew 19:6).[3] Tim Hegg puts it well:

> Instead of analyzing marriage and divorce from a detached, legal perspective of what things could legitimately dissolve the marriage covenant, Yeshua has emphasized the purpose of marriage, grounded as it is in the very creation of male and female, and as a revelation of God's own covenant faithfulness to His chosen people. Having made His perspective clear, and having put the emphasis upon marriage which accords with the Scriptures themselves, the obvious conclusion is that God hates divorce because it is contrary to Him and to His purposes.[4]

A noteworthy feature of Yeshua's answer to the Pharisees in regard to divorce is that He appeals to the original marriage between Adam

---

2   C.E.B. Cranfield, *The Bible and Christian Life* (T & T Clark, 1985), pp. 229-230

3   Yeshua does not rescind the Torah's permission to divorce, which was given by Moses "because of your hardness of heart." Due to our fallen world, God's laws governing divorce and remarriage are still needed to address situations that come about as a result of sin and disregard for God's will, as Yeshua Himself makes clear in verse 9.

4   Tim Hegg, *Commentary on the Gospel of Matthew* (Tacoma, WA: TorahResource, 2007) p. 827

and Eve as the ideal picture of what marriage is meant to be—a binding covenant established before God for His glory and purposes. On the basis of this original marriage, Yeshua declares of *all* marriages (which are to be modeled after the original), "So they are no longer *two* but one flesh." Yeshua's definition of marriage therefore assumed monogamy. When the apostle Paul cites Genesis 2:24 in his own teaching on marriage, he says the same thing: "Therefore a man shall leave his father and mother and hold fast to his wife, and the *two* shall become one flesh" (Ephesians 5:31). You'll notice that Yeshua and Paul say the *two* will become one flesh. They don't say three, four, or more. Two shall become one. Therefore, both Yeshua and Paul, who based their teachings on the ideal model of marriage as established in Genesis 2:24, define marriage as monogamous.

The fact that God designed the original marriage to be a monogamous union was not some arbitrary decision on His part. Marriage, as God established it, is deeply theological and rooted in biblical truths about His nature expressed in the Scriptures. Davidson writes, "Monogamy is ultimately rooted in monotheism and in the concept of *imago Dei* (image of God): just as the Lord God, who is 'one' (Deut. 6:4), is not involved in promiscuous relationships within a polytheistic pantheon, so husbands and wives, created in God's image, are to be monogamous in their marital relationship with each other."[5] If God's original design for marriage is meant to be a picture of His nature and character, then any deviation from God's original design could be said to be a distortion of that picture. As followers of the God of Israel, our purpose is to bear God's image, and that includes accurately

---

5   Richard M. Davidson, "Condemnation and Grace: Polygamy and Concubinage in the Old Testament," *Christian Research Journal*, Vol. 38, No. 5 (2015)

representing the character and nature of God by how we live our lives, especially in our marriages.

Someone might ask, "But if this issue is so important, why doesn't God give any commandments prohibiting polygamy?" This is a great question worth thoughtful consideration. If polygamy were so against God's will and design for marriage, wouldn't we expect God to make that clear in the Torah? After all, adultery and homosexuality likewise are distortions of God's original design for marriage, and thus, there are clear laws against those acts. But when it comes to polygamy, it's commonly believed that there is no direct commandment prohibiting it. Moreover, several passages throughout the Old Testament, on the surface, *seem* to permit and even approve of the practice. How do we deal with that?

In this chapter, I will argue the following four points:

1. Like homosexuality, polygamy is a clear deviation from God's original design for marriage as established in creation.

2. The Torah *does* in fact prohibit the practice of polygamy.

3. Rather than being endorsed in the Bible, polygamy is consistently painted in a negative light and thus discouraged throughout the Bible.

4. The passages in which polygamy might seem to be approved by God are misunderstood.

Regarding my first point, we've already seen through the creation account in Genesis that monogamy is God's original design for marriage. And again, we've seen that both Yeshua and Paul affirm this original design for marriage by using that established model as the basis for their own teachings on what marriage is intended to look like. While monogamy may not have been the focus of their teachings, it is nevertheless the assumed model in every mention of marriage throughout the New Testament. The Apostle Paul said, "[E]ach man should have his own wife and each woman her own husband" (1 Corinthians 7:2). Paul also said that elders and deacons within the congregation are to have only one wife, again reinforcing monogamy for everyone, as elders are to be examples of righteous living to the rest of the congregation (1 Timothy 3:2, 12). A prohibition of polygamy can also be logically deduced from Yeshua's statement that a man who divorces his wife without warrant and marries another woman "commits adultery" (Matthew 19:9). As Phillip Segal explains, Yeshua "would not call a divorced man's remarriage adultery, even if the divorce was not legitimate and he continued in the marital relationship to the first woman, if he was permitted a second wife."[6]

Yeshua and Paul weren't pulling this principle out of nowhere. Their teachings were based on the Torah, which entails that they interpreted the issue of polygamy as being prohibited according to the Torah. But where in the Torah does this idea come from? As stated earlier, God's original design for marriage is one man and one woman. Therefore, if the original marriage was typological for all marriages, as Yeshua and Paul understood it, then polygamy obviously goes against God's intent for marriage as established in the beginning.

Based on Yeshua's and Paul's appeal to the creation ideal in Genesis 1-2, we can therefore say that polygamy is against God's ideal will for marriage. Perhaps, like divorce, polygamy was *permitted* as a result of

---

6   Phillip Sigal, *The Halakhah of Jesus of Nazareth According to the Gospel of Matthew* (Atlanta, GA: Society of Biblical Literature, 2007), p. 114

human sin and the nature of our fallen world. Therefore, rather than directly prohibit it, God met humans where they were by allowing polygamy for a time in the hope that He could gradually guide them back toward the creation ideal. In the meantime, He gave regulations that prevented the mistreatment of women and children in these less-than-ideal situations (e.g. Deuteronomy 21:15-17). But again, God's ideal, which believers should strive to establish in their lives and world, is monogamy. This ideal is reaffirmed by both Yeshua's and Paul's implicit condemnation of polygamy in their teachings.

Does the Torah Prohibit Polygamy?
An Examination of Leviticus 18:18

Since the Messiah and the apostle Paul both reaffirm the creation ideal of monogamy, thus implicitly condemning polygamy, we should consider polygamy to be against God's will for marriage. However, there is something more to consider, which brings me to my next point: the Bible *does* in fact prohibit the practice of polygamy. To begin, consider this commandment in Leviticus:

> You shall not marry a woman in addition to her sister as a rival while she is alive, to uncover her nakedness. (Leviticus 18:18, NASB)

This verse is usually understood as prohibiting only one type of polygamous marriage, specifically a marriage to two sisters while both are alive. The implication of such an interpretation is that a man cannot marry his sister-in-law, but polygamy in general is permitted. However, some scholars have challenged this interpretation.[7] There

---

7   I am grateful for the work of Richard M. Davidson and Gordon P. Hugenberger, which

are reasons to think that this verse does not necessarily refer to two blood-related sisters but to two *women* in general. Thus, "sister" would have a broader definition that would include *any* woman and not just a blood relative. If this interpretation is correct, we therefore have a direct commandment in the Torah forbidding polygamy.

Evidence that some Jewish groups understood Leviticus 18:18 as a general prohibition against polygamy exists as early as the Qumran community, a first-century Jewish sect from whom we get the Dead Sea Scrolls.[8] For instance, among the Dead Sea Scrolls is what's known as The Temple Scroll, which contains a commentary on Deuteronomy 17:14-20 concerning kings. According to scholars,[9] this commentary appeals to Leviticus 18:18 as a proof text against the practice of polygamy:

> He may not take a wife from any of the nations. Rather, he must take himself a wife from his father's house—that is, from his father's family. **He is not to take another wife in addition to her; no, she alone shall be with him as long as she lives.** If she dies, then he may take himself another wife from his father's house, that is, his family. [Emphasis added][10]

has been very helpful to me in putting together the material in this section on Leviticus 18:18. See Richard M. Davidson, *Flame of Yahweh: Sexuality in the Old Testament* (Peabody, MA: Hendrickson Publishers, 2007), pp. 193-198; Gordon P. Hugenberger, *Marriage as a Covenant: A Study of Biblical Law and Ethics Governing Marriage, Developed from the Perspective of Malachi* (1994), pp. 115-118

8   The Temple Scroll (11Q Col. 57:17-19); The Damascus Document (CD 4:21; 5:1)

9   See David Instone Brewer, "Jesus' Old Testament Basis for Monogamy," *The Old Testament in the New Testament: Essays in Honour of J. L. North*. Steve Moyise, ed. (Sheffield Academic Press, 2000), pp. 80-89

10   Michael Wise, Marin Abegg & Edward Cook, "11QT57:15-19," *Dead Sea Scrolls: A New Translation* (New York, NY: HarperCollins Publishers, 1996) p. 485

In another writing from Qumran known as The Damascus Document, the sectarian community condemns the "Shoddy-Wall-Builders," which "may be a reference to the Pharisees or non-Qumran Jews in general."[11] The Qumran community charges their opponents with committing various sins, including polygamy:

> They are caught in two traps: fornication, by taking two wives
> in their lifetimes although the principle of creation is "male
> and female He created them" (Gen. 1:27).[12]

While the statement "taking two wives in their lifetimes" could be read as a prohibition against remarriage after divorce, scholars understand it to be a condemnation of polygamy and an allusion to Leviticus 18:18 ("And you shall not take a woman as a rival wife… while her sister is still alive").[13] The appeal to Genesis 1:27 parallels

---

11 See David Instone-Brewer, "Jesus' Old Testament Basis for Monogamy," *The Old Testament in the New Testament: Essays in Honour of J. L. North*. Steve Moyise, ed. (Sheffield Academic Press, 2000): "The 'wall' may be a reference to the 'fence' which the Pharisees put around the law (m. Abot. 1.1). The fence was the system of rabbinic laws which amplified and specified what the biblical law said and what it implied. By keeping all these rabbinic laws, one would by certain to fulfill all the biblical laws, so they were a 'fence' to protect one from trespassing a biblical law." (p. 81, n. 32)

12 Michael Wise, Marin Abegg & Edward Cook, "CD 4:20-21" *Dead Sea Scrolls: A New Translation* (New York, NY: HarperCollins Publishers, 1996) p. 55

13 See David Instone-Brewer, "Jesus' Old Testament Basis for Monogamy," *The Old Testament in the New Testament: Essays in Honour of J. L. North*. Steve Moyise, ed. (Sheffield Academic Press, 2000): "The law of Lev. 18.18 (according to the Qumran exegetes) concerns a man who has a wife and wants to take another, which is prohibited unless the first wife has died. If a man is divorced from his first wife, he no longer has a wife, so this law does not apply to him. We can see that this interpretation was in the minds of the Qumran exegetes in the way they summarize the teaching of Lev. 18.18 with the words 'taking two wives during their lives.' This phrase reminds the reader that

Yeshua's argument in Matthew 19:4-9, wherein He implicitly condemns polygamy on the basis of the same passage. Noting these similarities, David Instone-Brewer writes, "Jesus' teaching on monogamy echoed that found at Qumran, even so far as using the same proof texts and an identical introductory phrase. Both sources probably reflected a widely accepted teaching, though rabbinic Judaism did not forbid polygamy for several centuries."[14]

The Qumran community's interpretation of Leviticus 18:18 as being a prohibition against polygamy in general has caused some scholars to reexamine the biblical text itself to see if such a reading has warrant. In light of such investigations, one scholar by the name of Angelo Tosato has definitively declared, "Qumran's interpretation of Leviticus 18:18 is not only correct but even more faithful to the original sense than the interpretation commonly given today."[15] Can this assertion be justified? Why should we believe that Leviticus 18:18 prohibits *all* polygamy rather than simply prohibiting a marriage between a man and two literal sisters? Several points can be made to support this conclusion.

First, in Hebrew, "a woman in addition to her sister," is *ishah el-achotah*, which literally means "a woman to her sister." This is an idiomatic expression, which, as scholars like Richard Davidson and

---

Lev. 18.18 is emphatically speaking about being married to two wives at once [...] This explanation is confirmed considerable by the Qumran texts which show that divorce was permitted. Therefore this exegetical argument does not prohibit divorce or remarriage at Qumran, but is directed solely at the practice of polygamy which the Qumran exegetes considered to be unlawful." (pp. 85-86)

14   Ibid., p. 105. Instone-Brewer does mention that, while rabbinic Judaism did not officially prohibit polygamy until the eleventh century, polygamy had probably ceased to be practiced within Judaism long before this (p. 78).

15   Angelo Tosato, "The Law of Leviticus 18:18: A Reexamination," *CBQ* Vol. 46 (1984), p. 208

Gordon Hugenberger have argued, is always used in the distributive sense of "one in addition to another." Consider the following verses in which this exact phrase is used idiomatically:

> Five curtains shall be coupled to one another [*ishah el-achotah*], and the other five curtains shall be coupled to one another [*ishah el-achotah*]. (Exodus 26:3)

חֲמֵשׁ הַיְרִיעֹת תִּהְיֶיןָ חֹבְרֹת אִשָּׁה אֶל־אֲחֹתָהּ וְחָמֵשׁ יְרִיעֹת חֹבְרֹת אִשָּׁה
אֶל־אֲחֹתָהּ׃

> And you shall make fifty clasps of gold, and couple the curtains one to the other [*ishah el-achotah*] with the clasps, so that the tabernacle may be a single whole. (Exodus 26:6)

וְעָשִׂיתָ חֲמִשִּׁים קַרְסֵי זָהָב וְחִבַּרְתָּ אֶת־הַיְרִיעֹת אִשָּׁה אֶל־אֲחֹתָהּ בַּקְּרָסִים וְהָיָה
הַמִּשְׁכָּן אֶחָד׃ פ

> Their wings touched one another [*ishah el-achotah*]. Each one of them went straight forward, without turning as they went. (Ezekiel 1:9)

חֹבְרֹת אִשָּׁה אֶל־אֲחוֹתָהּ כַּנְפֵיהֶם לֹא־יִסַּבּוּ בְלֶכְתָּן אִישׁ אֶל־עֵבֶר פָּנָיו
יֵלֵכוּ׃

In Exodus 26, you'll notice that it speaks of the coupling of curtains and clasps "one to the other," which is literally, "a woman to her sister." The verse in Ezekiel speaks of the wings of the cherubim touching "one another," which, again, literally translates to "a woman to her sister." In Hebrew, this is *ishah el-achotah*, the exact same phrase used in Leviticus 18:18.

In fact, every time the phrase *ishah el-achotah* occurs in the Old Testament, it is used in an idiomatic manner, meaning "one to another."[16] This is also the case with the masculine equivalent of this phrase, *ish el-akiw*, which literally means, "a man to his brother." This expression, too, is used idiomatically in the distributive sense of "one in addition to another" in every occurrence.[17]

Thus, when we interpret the phrase *ishah el-achotah* in light of its consistent usage throughout the Scriptures, Leviticus 18:18 ought to be understood idiomatically and distributively as saying you shall not marry one woman in addition to another. Since this phrase is used in this way everywhere else in the Bible, it doesn't make sense to interpret Leviticus 18:18 as referring to literal sisters only. The word *sister* in Leviticus 18:18, therefore, ought to be understood broadly as a female in general.

Second, if the author of Leviticus intended Leviticus 18:18 to be understood as a prohibition against marrying literal sisters, thereby implicitly permitting polygamy in general, it would be very clear grammatically. But the textual evidence suggests something else. Old Testament scholar and professor, Gordon Hugenberger, explains that, if the intention of Leviticus 18:18 was to prohibit a man from marrying a woman and her sister, we would expect the use of the conjunction "and [ו]," rather than the preposition "to [אֶל]," so that the verse would say "a woman and her sister." This is the precise grammar of the phrase employed by the author in the preceding verse where he

---

16   Exodus 26:3, 5, 6, 17; Ezekiel 1:9, 23; 3:13

17   Genesis 37:19; 42:21, 28; Exodus 16:15; 25:20; 37:9; Numbers 14:4; 2 Kings 7:6; Jeremiah 13:14; 25:26; Ezekiel 24:23; 33:30

prohibits sexual relations with "a woman *and* her daughter." According to Hugenberger, "It appears likely that it was the awareness of this usage which already led the Zadokites and the Qumran community in the first century B.C., as well as the much later Karaites, to interpret Lev. 18:18 as an explicit prohibition against polygyny."[18]

In other words, the fact that the verse uses the phrase "a woman *in addition to* her sister," employing the preposition "to" rather than the conjunction "and," lends support to the theory that this phrase is intended to be understood idiomatically in the distributive sense rather than merely prohibiting someone from marrying two literal sisters. If it were referring to two literal sisters, we would expect the phrasing of the verse to be consistent with the other anti-incest laws of Leviticus 18, but it isn't. Instead, it uses "a common expression that did not refer to relatives, except by coincidence."[19]

Third, the fact that Leviticus 18:18 prohibits polygamy in general is made all the more clear when we consider the reason for the commandment, which is to prevent rivalry between the two wives: "You shall not marry a woman in addition to her sister *as a rival*" (Leviticus 18:18). This consequence applies to any type of polygamous union, not merely that of a marriage with two literal sisters. As Tosato remarks:

> This motivation shows that the act legislated against is deemed criminal, not in itself (and thus it is not a case of an incestuous union; nor more generally of a sexual union retained

---

18   Gordon P. Hugenberger, *Marriage as a Covenant: A Study of Biblical Law and Ethics Governing Marriage, Developed from the Perspective of Malachi* (1994), pp. 115-116

19   Jay Sklar, *Tyndale Old Testament Commentaries: Leviticus* (Downers Grove, IL: IVP Academic), p. 235

intrinsically perverse), **but is deemed criminal in relation to the man's first wife** who would be damaged. In addition, the harm which the law wants avoided is such (rivalry, enmity) that any woman (and not necessarily a sister of the first wife) is capable of causing. [emphasis added][20]

Indeed, if the reason for this commandment was to avoid rivalry between co-wives, it doesn't make sense that this law should be limited to literal sisters. Throughout history, we've seen the contentious relationship between co-wives, whether they were sisters or not. You need to look no further than Abraham's wives, Sarah and Hagar, to see this. Moreover, the very same language, "as a rival," used in Leviticus 18:18, is also used in 1 Samuel 1:6 in regard to the contentious relationship between Peninnah and Hannah, the wives of Elkanah (1 Samuel 1:6)—and there's no evidence that these women were literal sisters. Think about it: why would there be rivalry and strife in a polygamous relationship *only* if the wives were sisters? The rivalry and strife are due to women competing for the attention and love from the same man. Would only sisters experience such rivalry? Of course not.

Thus, the type of marriage that is forbidden in Leviticus 18:18 is likely to create rivalry between the wives, which "was typical between wives of the same man (Gen. 16:4; 29:21-30:24; 1 Sam. 1:6), a point highlighted in these stories in order to stress again that such marriages should be avoided."[21] Since such rivalry can be created in any polyg-

---

20   Angelo Tosato, "The Law of Leviticus 18:18: A Reexamination," *CBQ* Vol. 46 (1984), p. 207

21   Jay Sklar, *Tyndale Old Testament Commentaries: Leviticus* (Downers Grove, IL: IVP Academic), p. 236

amous marriage, not just a marriage with two literal sisters, we ought to view Leviticus 18:18 as a prohibition against polygamy in general.

Fourth, unlike the anti-incest laws in the same chapter, Leviticus 18:18 contains a time limitation. As Davidson explains, the command against taking *ishah el-achotah* "applies only while the first one is alive. This is in stark contrast to the laws dealing with nearness of kin, which have no such temporary limitation."[22]

Fifth, the overall literary structure of Leviticus 18 suggests that this is a law prohibiting polygamy in general since it is not part of the same unit of laws as the anti-incest laws. Some people insist that Leviticus 18:18 is dealing with a specific incestuous union involving two literal sisters since it occurs directly after many other laws forbidding various incestuous relations. However, scholars have pointed out that there is a major literary break between verse 17 and 18 in Leviticus 18. Leviticus 18 presents two separate units of laws—the first unit dealing specifically with laws prohibiting various incestuous relationships and the second unit dealing with laws governing sexual morality more generally. Leviticus 18:18 is part of the *second* unit and therefore not intended to be included with the anti-incest laws of verses 6-17. As Paul Copan explains:

> Each verse in 7-17 begins identically, starting with the noun
> "the nakedness (of) [*erwat*]," and it leads up to the command,
> "You shall not uncover _____'s nakedness." Also, in each
> of these verses (except v. 9) an explanation is given for the
> prohibition (e.g., "she is your mother"); this explanation isn't
> found in verse 18, which we would expect if it were an incest

---

22   Richard M. Davidson, *Flame of Yahweh: Sexuality in the Old Testament* (Peabody, MA: Hendrickson Publishers, 2007), pp. 196

prohibition. By contrast, each verse in 18-23 begins with a different construction. Even if you don't read Hebrew, you can truly just glance at the text and immediately see the difference in structure starting with verse 18. Verses 18-23 each begin with what's called the *waw* conjunctive (like our word "and") followed by a different word than "nakedness" (*erwat*); also, instead of the consistent use of the negative (*lo*) plus the verb "uncover" (*tegalleh*, from the root *galah*), as in 7-17, here the negative particles are used before verbs other than uncover. **Why are these contrasts important? In verses 6-17, we're dealing with** *kinship bonds* **while verses 18-23 address prohibited sexual relations** *outside of kinship bonds*. [Emphasis added][23]

All of this leads to the conclusion that Leviticus 18:18 refers to *any* two women and not merely two literal sisters. Thus, Leviticus 18:18 prohibits a man from marrying another woman in addition to his first wife while she is alive. In other words, the Torah directly prohibits polygamy. This, of course, aligns with God's original design for marriage as established in creation.

That being said, even if some insist that Leviticus 18:18 refers specifically to two literal sisters, it still wouldn't necessarily follow that polygamy in general is morally permitted. For instance, Leviticus 19:29 prohibits a man from making his daughter a prostitute. The fact that this commandment specifically refers to a daughter gives no implicit permission for a man to make *other* women, such as his wife

---

23   Paul Copan, *Is God a Moral Monster?: Making Sense of the Old Testament God* (Grand Rapids, MI: Baker Publishing Group, 2011), p. 113

or sister, prostitutes. Likewise, there's simply no reason to assume any kind of implicit permission of polygamy in Leviticus 18:18.

Some might raise the objection that Leviticus 18:18 cannot be a prohibition against polygamy in general because there is no legal punishment for having more than one wife. While it's true that the Torah doesn't mention any legal consequences for practicing polygamy, the commandment against polygamy is certainly not unique in that regard. For instance, there is no legal punishment for hating someone, despite the fact that Leviticus 19:17 says, "You shall not hate your brother in your heart." Also, the tenth commandment prohibits coveting, but the Torah likewise gives no civil punishment for breaking this law. Nobody would suggest that the lack of legal punishments for transgressing these commandments invalidates them.

So why does polygamy go unpunished within the Torah legal system despite its being morally condemned by God? Hugenberger suggests that "Leviticus 18:18 can be categorized as a *lex imperfecta*, a law which prohibits something without thereby rendering it invalid (reflecting a society which would have lacked the requisite means of enforcement in any case)."[24] In other words, practically speaking, carrying out a civil punishment for transgressing this law would have been difficult to enforce in the ancient world. So we can say that the Torah morally prohibits polygamy but, at the same time, tolerates it from a civil standpoint in the sense that it provides no penalties for transgressing the commandment. Whatever the reason may be, the fact that there are no legal consequences for transgressing God's law against polygamy certainly gives no basis for rejecting the law from a moral standpoint. And on that note, the fact that there is no punishment for

---

24   Gordon P. Hugenberger, *Marriage as a Covenant: A Study of Biblical Law and Ethics Governing Marriage, Developed from the Perspective of Malachi* (1994), p. 118

transgressing Leviticus 18:18 actually further distinguishes it from the anti-incest laws. Leviticus 20 reiterates the anti-incest laws of Leviticus 18 and lists the punishments for transgressing them. However, the commandment in Leviticus 18:18 is absent, perhaps indicating that it is not merely another form of incest but a law against polygamy in general.

In conclusion, there are several reasons to think that the Qumran community's interpretation of Leviticus 18:18 as being a general prohibition against polygamy is correct. Like homosexuality and adultery in the scope of sexual relationships, polygamy is a deviation from the creation ideal. Therefore, we shouldn't be surprised to find a commandment in the Torah that prohibits it.

The Divine Disapproval of Polygamy

Given that polygamy is a deviation from the creation ideal in addition to being morally prohibited in the Torah, it really shouldn't surprise us to discover that polygamy, rather than being endorsed, is painted in a negative light throughout the Bible. Based on what has been established so far, those who practiced polygamy throughout biblical history were doing so in direct violation of not only God's original design for marriage exemplified in creation but also of a direct commandment in the Torah. In addition to these specific moral and legal statements, the biblical authors teach against polygamy via narrative clues revealing the disastrous consequences of this practice. As Davidson remarks:

> In the patriarchal period, there are several biblical examples
> of plural marriages. Although these biblical narratives provide
> no explicit verbal condemnation of this practice, **the narra-**
> **tor presents each account in such a way as to underscore**

a theology of disapproval. The record of these polygamous relationships bristles with discord, rivalry, heartache, and even rebellion, revealing the motivations and/or disastrous consequences that invariably accompanied such departures from God's Edenic ideal." [emphasis added][25]

The first recorded polygamist in the Bible is Lamech, a man who lived a life of violence and vengeance (Genesis 4:23-24). Lamech was a descendent of Cain, who likewise was a murderer and rebel against God. This is where Scripture says the practice of polygamy originated, and this family is certainly not one that Scripture encourages us to emulate.

Aside from Lamech, there are a few more stories in Scripture about those who chose to be polygamists, which often produced disastrous consequences. For instance, Abram's polygamy, which ultimately came about from a lack of faith in God's promises, resulted in severe strife and contention between Sarai and Hagar as well as between Isaac and Ishmael. Some scholars suggest that there may even be a literary parallel between Abram's polygamy with Sarai and Hagar and the fall of Adam and Eve in Genesis 3.[26] For instance, Genesis 3:6 says that Eve "took"—*laqach*—the fruit from the tree and "gave" it—*nathan*—to Adam. Likewise, Genesis 16:3 says that Sarai "took"—*laqach*—her servant Hagar and "gave"—*nathan*—her to Abram. Also consider Genesis 3:17, which says that Adam "listened to the voice of" his wife. Likewise, in Genesis 16:2 it says that Abram "listened to the voice of" his wife, Sarai. Identical Hebrew words and expressions are used in the

---

25   Richard M. Davidson, *Flame of Yahweh: Sexuality in the Old Testament* (Peabody, MA: Hendrickson Publishers, 2007), pp. 180

26   Ibid., p. 185

same order in both accounts. These parallels have led some scholars to conclude that the biblical author was intentionally connecting the Hagar scandal with the fall of Adam and Eve. In other words, Abram's polygamy is portrayed as the "fall" of Abram and Sarai just like Adam and Eve fell in the Garden. Hagar, as the second woman, was the forbidden fruit.

As we move forward to Jacob's narrative, we see that his polygamy likewise results in constant strife, contention, deception, and jealousy within his very dysfunctional family. Again, we see with Jacob a clear picture of the negative affects of turning away from God's creation ideal for marriage. Davidson writes, "That the narrator is not presenting polygamy in a favorable light is apparent from the depiction of the tensions within the family. God's disapproval is shouting at us, as it were, from every detail of the disastrous results of the polygamous union."[27]

The Bible records that when Esau was forty years old, he likewise became a polygamist. Esau's wives "made life bitter for Isaac and Rebecca" (Genesis 26:34-35). Hebrews 12:16 says that Esau had a "sexually immoral and unholy" character, so it's not surprising to see that he deviated from God's design for marriage by being a polygamist.

Sometimes the judge Gideon, who is said to have had "many wives" in Judges 8:30, is offered as an example of God's endorsement of polygamy. While it's true that Gideon is given as an example of faith in Hebrews 11:32, there is no reason to assume that God endorsed every aspect of his character and deeds. In fact, a major theme of the Book of Judges is that "every man did what was right in his own eyes." As J.K. McKee notes, "This is something that influences almost everything one

---

27 Ibid., p. 187

reads in Judges, and should not be underemphasized."[28] The biblical author's point is to condemn the idolatry and sexual immorality of the times, and he did that by recording all the ugly details and catastrophic results of sin. Gideon is no exception. Gideon's pride and idolatry later in life contributed to Israel's downslide into apostasy, which reached its climax with Abimelech, one of Gideon's sons who had his seventy siblings murdered (Judges 9:5). According to McKee, "There is no reason for us to doubt that Gideon's polygamy was connected with the spiraling down of Israel's religious environment."[29]

Perhaps the most obvious example of the awful consequences of polygamy is King Solomon, who married 700 women and had 300 concubines. Solomon's polygamy was in direct opposition to the commandment given to kings in Deuteronomy 17:17 not to multiply wives, which we'll unpack in more detail a little later. The biblical author is clear that Solomon's idolatry and eventual downfall were the direct result of his polygamy:

> He had 700 wives, who were princesses, and 300 concubines.
> **And his wives turned away his heart. For when Solomon**
> **was old his wives turned away his heart after other gods**,
> and his heart was not wholly true to the Lord His God, as
> was the heart of David his father. (1 Kings 11:3-4, emphasis
> added)

Solomon married many foreign women, and those foreign women knew other gods, which appears to have influenced Solomon to also

---

28 J.K. McKee, *Men and Women in the Body of Messiah: Answering Crucial Questions* (Richardson, TX: Messianic Apologetics, 2018), p. 291
29 Ibid., p. 292

go after other gods. Again, the biblical author seems to intentionally associate polygamy with disaster.

Some might object to these examples and insist that the contention, heartache, rebellion, etc., were not *because* of polygamy. I am not suggesting that other negative factors weren't involved, but the fact that polygamy always seems to accompany these disastrous situations doesn't seem to be a coincidence on the part of the biblical authors. Again, as Davidson suggests, "Although these biblical narratives provide no explicit verbal condemnation of this practice, the narrator presents each account in such a way as to underscore a theology of disapproval."[30]

The negative consequences that have accompanied the practice of polygamy throughout Israel's history perhaps contribute to the Jewish people all but abandoning the practice by the first century. Instone-Brewer notes that polygamy "was not widespread and it was already declining in the first century," and that "there was already an established feeling that polygamy was inappropriate and some groups taught that it was not permitted by Scripture."[31] While polygamy wasn't officially prohibited by rabbinic Judaism until the eleventh century, "it had probably ceased to be practiced long before this."[32] As biblical scholar and rabbi, J.H. Hertz, remarks:

> Polygamy seems to have wellnigh disappeared in Israel after
> the Babylonian Exile. Early Rabbinic literature presupposes

---

30   Richard M. Davidson, *Flame of Yahweh: Sexuality in the Old Testament* (Peabody, MA: Hendrickson Publishers, 2007), p. 180

31   David Instone-Brewer, "Jesus' Old Testament Basis for Monogamy," *The Old Testament in the New Testament: Essays in Honour of J. L. North*. Steve Moyise, ed. (Sheffield Academic Press, 2000), pp. 104-105

32   Ibid., p. 78

a practically monogamic society; and out of 2,800 Teachers mentioned in the Talmudim, one is only stated to have had two wives. In the fourth century Aramaic paraphrase (Targum) of the Book of Ruth, the kinsman (IV, 6) refuses to "redeem" Ruth, saying, "**I cannot marry her, because I am already married; I have no right to take an additional wife, lest it lead to strife in my home.**" Such paraphrase would be meaningless if it did not reflect the general feeling of the people on this question. [Emphasis added][33]

Something important to note here is that the Targum specifically mentions that the kinsman could not marry because he was already married. Not only that, but his further reasoning is, "lest it lead to strife in my home." This language is similar to Leviticus 18:18, in which marrying another woman would cause rivalry between the wives.

In conclusion, polygamy is seen to be repeatedly discouraged throughout the Old Testament. It's no wonder that some sects of Judaism in the first century, such as the Qumran community, fiercely opposed the practice. It is also no wonder that the apostolic instruction in the first century consistently upholds monogamy as God's ideal for marriage.

What About Concubines?

Before moving on to the next point, it's important to address the issue of concubines since it is related to this topic. It was not uncommon in the ancient world for men to have concubines in addition to

---

33   J.H. Hertz, *Pentateuch & Haftorahs* (London: The Soncino Press, 1960), p. 932, quoted in J.K. McKee, *Men and Women in the Body of Messiah: Answering Crucial Questions* (Richardson, TX: Messianic Apologetics, 2018)

wives, and we even see some men in the Bible who practiced concubinage. Sometimes the term concubine (*piylegesh*) refers to a legitimate wife whom a man marries after the death of his first wife. This is the case with Keturah, who is called Abraham's "wife" in Genesis 25:1 but his "concubine" in 1 Chronicles 1:32. However, most of the time, this term refers to a woman who could be taken by a man without any legal formalization. She would often voluntarily sell herself as a maidservant to a family for the purpose of the man's sexual pleasure as well as to bear children in the case of barrenness. We see this with Jacob, who had two concubines, Bilhah and Zilpah, in addition to his wives, Rachel and Leah. In the ancient world, a concubine did not have the same legal status as a full and legitimate wife.

Many of the arguments given in this chapter to demonstrate God's disapproval of polygamy can apply to concubinage also. For instance: 1) The ideal established in creation is one man and one woman, which certainly precludes multiple sexual partners at the same time, whether or not they are regarded as official "wives" in the eyes of ancient Near Eastern society. 2) In regard to Leviticus 18:18, one of the primary reasons for the command was to prevent the rivalry and strife that occurs when women compete for attention and love from the same man. Any sexual relationship with multiple women is likely to result in such rivalry. Thus, the harm that the Law wants to prevent certainly would apply to concubinage as well as to polygamy. 3) Concubinage usually appears right alongside polygamy as being painted in a negative light throughout the Bible and therefore appears to be intentionally discouraged by the biblical authors. Thus, like polygamy, concubinage is against God's will. The difference is that concubinage could actually be classified as a type of fornication—that is, "unlawful sexual activity," which would, by definition, include sexual relations outside of the marriage covenant. As discussed in the previous chapter, the sexual union is to be enjoyed only within the boundaries of a committed covenant relationship between husband and wife. The practice of concubinage, therefore, violates the sacredness of the sexual union between husband and wife.

Addressing the Passages That Allegedly Approve of Polygamy

A number of passages are often cited in support of the assertion that God morally permits or perhaps even endorses the practice of polygamy. My contention, however, is that these passages have been misunderstood. When we read them in context, we find that they in no way suggest that God approves of this practice.

The first passage we'll look at is Exodus 21:7-11. This passage concerns the "selling of a young woman to a family as an intended wife for either the man or for his son (vs. 7-9), in a kind of indentured servitude vis-à-vis an arranged marriage for a family that is destitute and needs a daughter provided for."[34] This was a common practice in the ancient Near East that the Torah permitted and regulated in the best interests of the maidservant:

> When a man sells his daughter as a slave, she shall not go out as the male slaves do. If she does not please her master, who has designated her for himself, then he shall let her be redeemed. He shall have no right to sell her to a foreign people, since he has broken faith with her. If he designates her for his son, he shall deal with her as with a daughter. **If he takes another wife to himself**, he shall not diminish her food, her

---

34   J.K. McKee, *Men and Women in the Body of Messiah: Answering Crucial Questions* (Richardson, TX: Messianic Apologetics, 2018), pp. 273-274.

clothing, or her marital rights. And if he does not do these three things for her, she shall go out for nothing, without payment of money. (Exodus 21:7-11, emphasis added)

There is certainly a lot of confusion when it comes to this passage. First, when the passage speaks of the man taking "another wife to himself," it is assumed that this refers to another wife *in addition to* the young maidservant mentioned previously in the passage. Thus, it is argued that this passage permits polygamy. However, when you carefully read through the passage, these laws have nothing to do with polygamy at all. A plain reading of the text reveals that these laws regard what is to be done when an engagement falls through.

To summarize: if the master decides not to marry the maidservant, the first solution is that she can be redeemed—that is, bought back. Alternatively, she and the master's son could get married. If that happens, then the master is to treat her not as a servant but as his daughter. If she is not redeemed, and if she doesn't marry the master's son, and if the master decides to marry someone else other than her, the master is still required to meet her basic needs. If he doesn't provide what she needs, the maidservant is able to leave and be considered a free woman.

These instructions are all about looking after the best interests of the maidservant so that she doesn't end up on the street if engagement plans fall through between her and her master. Again, it has nothing to do with polygamy. Some have argued, however, that the maidservant's "marital rights" with which her master must provide her refer to conjugal rights—that is, sexual pleasure—and thus this entails polygamy. While this interpretation is reflected in many English Bible translations, some scholars have challenged that understanding. The difficulty is that the Hebrew word *onah*, translated as "marital rights," is notoriously difficult to translate due to the fact that it is found only once in the entire Bible. Paul Copan argues that "shelter" or possibly "oil" are more accurate alternatives to "marital rights":

> The problem with the translation "marital rights" (*onah*) is this: It's a stab in the dark with a term *used only once* in the Old Testament. Words occurring once can often be tricky to handle, and translators should tread carefully. Some scholars have suggested more likely possibilities. For example, this word could be related to a word for oil (or possibly ointments) [...] However, an even more plausible rendering is available. The root of the word is associated with the idea of habitation or dwelling (*ma'on, me'onah*); for example, "God is a dwelling place," or heaven is God's holy "dwelling place" (Deut. 33:27; 2 Cron. 30:27). We can more confidently conclude that quarters or shelter (though possibly oil) are in view here, not conjugal rights. So the servant girl should be guaranteed the basic necessities: food, clothing, and lodging/shelter.[35]

Another objection is that this passage mentions the master having a "son." Therefore, it is argued that he must be married and is looking into getting a second wife. However, that assumption oversteps the textual evidence. Other reasonable options are that the master's first wife had passed away or he is divorced. There is no reason to assume polygamy here.

The second passage we'll look at is Deuteronomy 17:17, which is among the laws given to kings of Israel:

---

35   Paul Copan, *Is God a Moral Monster?: Making Sense of the Old Testament God* (Grand Rapids, MI: Baker Publishing Group, 2011), p. 115

And he shall not acquire many wives for himself, lest his heart turn away, nor shall he acquire for himself excessive silver and gold. (Deuteronomy 17:17)

The command not to "acquire many wives" is often interpreted as a prohibition against marrying an excessive number of women, but implicitly permitting polygamy for kings on a moderate level. In other words, it's said that a king is allowed to marry multiple women, just not too many. When this verse is taken in isolation, due to the imprecise language used, there isn't enough evidence to say that this verse prohibits polygamy. However, when we read this verse in its immediate context, a reasonable case can be made against polygamy:

And when he sits on the throne of his kingdom, **he shall write for himself in a book a copy of this law**, approved by the Levitical priests. And it shall be with him, and **he shall read in it all the days of his life**, that he may learn to fear the Lord his God by **keeping all the words of this law and these statutes, and doing them**, that his heart may not be lifted up above his brothers, and that **he may not turn aside from the commandment**, either to the right hand or the left, so that he may continue long in his kingdom, he and his children, in Israel. (Deuteronomy 17:18-20, emphasis added)

Just like his fellow citizens, the king was to follow the Torah. He was to write his own copy of the Torah and study it that He may not turn from God's commandments. And, of course, as established earlier in this chapter, one of God's commandments prohibits polygamy (Leviticus 18:18)! Since the king's righteous behavior was to serve as an example to the nation of Israel, it's therefore reasonable to conclude that Deuteronomy 17:17 upholds the similar prohibition against polygamy given to all of God's people. Furthermore, since the intent of these commandments was so that the king would not think of himself as superior to other Israelites or think of himself as above God's Law, the language used in verse 17 to "not acquire many wives for himself" ought to be understood in that light. That is, the king is prohibited from having more wives than regular Israelites were allowed to have—namely, more than one.

Now, if the intention of this verse was to prohibit *all* polygamy, some might say that it should be clearer. But as Hugenberger explains, "Given the undeniable right to remarry following divorce or the death of a spouse, however, the expression as it exists in 17:17 may be deemed adequate."[36] In other words, insisting that the language in verse 17 ought to be more precise in its prohibition of polygamy doesn't take into account a person's right to take another wife after divorce or the death of their first spouse. Therefore, the language in verse 17 allows for that right while also prohibiting polygamy.

Another passage that is often cited in support of polygamy is Deuteronomy 21:15-17, which details inheritance rights within a polygamous family:

> If a man has two wives, the one loved and the other unloved,
> and both the loved and the unloved have borne him children,
> and if the firstborn son belongs to the unloved, then on the
> day when he assigns his possessions as an inheritance to his
> sons, he may not treat the son of the loved as the firstborn in

---

36   Gordon P. Hugenberger, *Marriage as a Covenant: A Study of Biblical Law and Ethics Governing Marriage, Developed from the Perspective of Malachi* (1994), p. 120, n. 136

preference to the son of the unloved, who is the firstborn, but
he shall acknowledge the firstborn, the son of the unloved,
by giving him a double portion of all that he has, for he is
the firstfruits of his strength. The right of the firstborn is his.
(Deuteronomy 21:15-17)

It is claimed that, since this law regulates a polygamous union,
God therefore approves of polygamy. However, that is an unreasonable
assumption. For instance, the Torah provides laws for restitution to
address the negative consequences of stealing. The existence of such
laws do not legitimize theft. Deuteronomy 23:18 forbids prostitute
wages from being used as payment of vows, but the existence of this
law certainly doesn't legitimize prostitution. Thus, in the same way, the
existence of a law detailing the rights of the firstborn in a less-than-
ideal situation—that is, when a man has two wives—doesn't legitimize
polygamy.

Another passage that is often cited as an example of God's approval
of polygamy is Deuteronomy 25:5-10, the law of levirate marriage.
This law states that when a husband dies childless, his brother or near
relative is to marry the deceased husband's widow in order that the
firstborn from this marriage would be the legal heir of the deceased
husband. It is argued that, since this passage does not explicitly exempt
a married brother from his levirate duty, it's *theoretically* possible that
this law would require a married brother to take an additional wife.

It could certainly be argued that this possibility exists in theory,
but when we look at how this law is carried out *in practice*, we see
something different. For instance, we see the practice of levirate
marriage being employed only two times in the Bible—with Tamar
and Ruth. In both cases, they were remarried to men who did not
already have a wife.

It's important also to understand that this law was not given in a vacuum; it ought to be understood in light of everything else the Torah says on the subject. For instance, this law has clear exemptions, even if they aren't explicitly stated. For instance, when Tamar's husband Onan died, she was told to remain a widow until Onan's brother Shelah was old enough to marry her. But an exemption for age is never stated in the law. We can reasonably conclude, therefore, that there could be other exemptions even if they aren't explicitly stated in the passage. And since the Torah likely prohibits polygamy in Leviticus 18:18, we can reasonably conclude that this law exempts married relatives from this duty.

Admittedly, since the passage does not exhaustively cover every single situation in which the levirate duty may or may not apply, someone *could* argue that polygamy is permitted. However, that conclusion appears least likely. *At most*, it's the rare exception to the rule and permitted only in extremely specific circumstances. This could be compared to the principle that breaking the Sabbath is allowed in order to save the life of a person or animal. Those specific situations in which breaking the Sabbath might be necessary to save a life do not give permission for breaking the Sabbath in general. Likewise, while it's theoretically possible that polygamy might be permitted in extremely rare circumstances, that possibility certainly doesn't entail that polygamy ought to be approved in any other situation.

In summary, the law of levirate marriage needs to be understood in light of everything else the Bible says on the topic. And since the Bible is clear that polygamy is against God's will, it's reasonable to conclude that married relatives would be exempt from levirate duty. But even if the law of levirate marriage allows for polygamy, it is, at most, the rare exception to the rule in a specific situation. Thus, the law of levirate marriage doesn't give approval for polygamy in general.

Another passage cited in support of polygamy is Numbers 12:1. Moses is alleged to have had two wives at the same time. It is argued that Moses couldn't have given commandments from God prohibiting polygamy since he was practicing it himself. But is this true? The suggestion that Moses was a polygamist is based on an assumption that Moses' wife, Zipporah, a Midianite (Exodus 2:21; 4:25; 18:2), is a different woman than the "Cushite woman" mentioned in Numbers 12:1. However, it's more likely that the Cushite woman actually refers to Zipporah herself. John Rea writes:

> It is possible that Zipporah, a Midianite, was also designated a Cushite, for Midian included part of NW Arabia where some Cushite tribes lived. Furthermore, she may have been called a Cushite because her complexion may have been darker than that of most Israelites.[37]

This conclusion can be further confirmed in Habakkuk 3:7. As John Walton points out, Cushan and Midian occur in synonymous parallelism in this verse, suggesting that the terms referred to the same region. This gives "credence to the identity of the Cushite woman with Zipporah."[38]

The issue in Numbers 12 is likely that Miriam and Aaron called Zipporah a derogatory name because, according to the following verse, they were frustrated with Moses' leadership and likely jealous of the influence that Zipporah had over Moses as his wife. Calling her a "Cushite woman" was an attempt to demean and depersonalize

---

37   John Rea, "Zipporah," *Wycliffe Bible Encyclopedia* (1975)

38   John Walton, *NIV Cultural Backgrounds Study Bible: Bringing to Life the Ancient World of Scripture* (Grand Rapids, MI: Zondervan, 2016), p. 252

Zipporah and therefore bring indictment against Moses for marrying a non-Hebrew. Whatever the case may be, the text certainly doesn't prove that Moses had more than one wife at the same time.

Another supposed biblical endorsement of polygamy is the example of King David. It is argued that since King David, a "man after God's own heart," practiced polygamy, then God must approve of the practice. However, there are several reasons to reject that reasoning.

First, when God anointed David as the future king and called him "a man after his own heart" in 1 Samuel 13:14, David was not yet a polygamist and was likely still single. Moreover, everyone knows that David fell into grievous sins, including adultery and murder. So this statement certainly does not imply an endorsement of *all* of David's behavior, and therefore it cannot be used to suggest that God approved of David's polygamy.

Many point to 2 Samuel 12, in which God sent Nathan with a message of reproof to David. It is claimed that Nathan's word makes it clear that God approved of David's polygamy:

> Nathan said to David, "You are the man! Thus says the Lord, the God of Israel, 'I anointed you king over Israel, and I delivered you out of the hand of Saul. **And I gave you your master's house and your master's wives into your arms** and gave you the house of Israel and of Judah. And if this were too little, I would add to you as much more. (2 Samuel 12:7-8, emphasis added)

A common argument goes like this: "See, God *gave* David Saul's wives! How can God be against polygamy if He gave David multiple wives Himself?" However, this argument has several problems. First, why do we assume that God's "giving" of Saul's wives to David entails that David married them? It's more likely that God's giving of Saul's house and wives into David's arms merely speaks of Saul's estate being transferred to David's care. Nothing in the text indicates marriage at all.

Second, just a few verses later (2 Samuel 12:11), God says that he will "give" *David's* wives to David's neighbor, who would then sleep with them. As the rest of the narrative details, this "neighbor" to whom God would give David's wives turned out to be David's son, Absalom. Now, Absalom's sleeping with David's wives was not only adultery but also incest. Therefore, if we're going to say that God's "giving" of Saul's wives to David is an endorsement of polygamy—assuming that David married Saul's wives—then that same logic could be used to say that God's "giving" of David's wives to Absalom is an endorsement of incest and adultery!

Third, David couldn't have married Saul's wives because, in addition to violating God's law against polygamy, he'd also be violating an anti-incest law. As we see in 1 Samuel 14:50, one of Saul's wives was Ahinoam, who was the mother of David's wife, Michal. Leviticus 18:17 prohibits marrying one's mother-in-law. Thus, the example of King David does not give any support to the idea that God approves of polygamy.

Another argument in support of the belief that God approves of polygamy is that God Himself is portrayed as a polygamist. This claim is based on Ezekiel 23, which is an allegory in which God is represented as being married to two sisters who represent the divided kingdom of Israel—Oholah, which represents Samaria, and Oholibah, which represents Jerusalem. The point of this allegory was to illustrate *all* of Israel's sin and unfaithfulness to God. Pointing to this allegory as a proof-text for polygamy, however, is missing the point. More-over, the symbolic marriage between God and Israel began long before

Israel was divided into two kingdoms. *All* of Israel is to be regarded as one people chosen by God. Not only that, but Ezekiel also speaks of these two kingdoms reuniting as one (Ezekiel 37:22). Thus, God and Israel's relationship is "monogamous," despite the temporary division of the nation. Ezekiel's allegorical message was one that addressed Israel's specific situation at the time, but from God's perspective and plan, His people are one.

The final argument we'll consider might go something like this: "Despite the fact that the practice of polygamy obviously seems to be condemned in the Bible, God nevertheless continued to bless and work through practicing polygamists such as Abraham, Jacob, and King David! So maybe the practice isn't ideal, but you can't really say that it's against God's will, can you?"

The answer is yes. The fact that God worked through fallen people—and indeed continues to work through every believer despite our many flaws—is not an argument that God approves of the behavior. It's a testament to His amazing grace and mercy *despite* their behavior (Romans 8:28). In the midst of an imperfect situation caused by people going against His will, we see that God took special care to protect the victims of polygamy, such as Hagar and Ishmael. God even gave laws looking out for the best interests of the children born in polygamous families, such as the firstborn son born to the polygamous parents in Deuteronomy 21. Indeed, the nation of Israel itself was born from the twelve sons of Jacob who were the products of polygamy.

God is certainly able to work within an imperfect situation in order to bring about His purposes. God does not abandon His people, but that does not stop Him from calling us back to His standard of holiness—especially in regard to His design for marriage. Again, God's compassion for the polygamist no more justifies polygamy than His compassion for the thief justifies theft. God is merciful, but He calls us to repentance.

In conclusion, we've established that polygamy is a clear deviation from God's original design for marriage as established in creation. Yeshua and the apostle Paul both clearly reaffirm the creation ideal of monogamy. We've established several good reasons to believe that the Torah *does* directly prohibit the practice of polygamy in Leviticus 18:18. We've established that polygamy is painted in a negative light and discouraged throughout the Bible. And finally, we've established that the passages often cited as evidence that polygamy is approved by God have been misunderstood. Therefore, no, God does not endorse polygamy.

CHAPTER 3
UNDERSTANDING THE TEST FOR ADULTERY

The act of adultery fundamentally damages marriage at its most basic level, whether or not that marriage is dissolved in the aftermath. While God can and has healed countless marriages in which adultery has occurred, it's extremely difficult to rebuild trust and intimacy between spouses when one or both have been unfaithful.[1] Moreover, adultery is an offense not only against one's spouse/family but also against God and the community. Why is adultery an offense against God? Because humans bear God's image, and adultery, like any sin, distorts that image. Also, God deeply cares about humans, and therefore it hurts Him when we hurt each other. Why is adultery an offense against the community? Because it's a threat to the social stability of the community. Here is how Dennis Prager eloquently puts it:

> Adultery threatens the building block of the civilization the Ten Commandments seek to create. That building block is family [...] Why is the family so important? Because without it, social stability is impossible. Because without it, the passing on of society's values from generation to generation is impossible. Because commitment to a spouse and children makes men and women more responsible and mature. Because the family

---

1   Infidelity is cited as the most common reported cause of divorce. See Paul Amato and Denise Previti, "People's Reasons for Divorcing: Gender, Social Class, the Life Course, and Adjustment," *Journal of Family Issues*, Vol. 24, No. 5 (2003), pp. 602-626

meets most people's deepest emotional needs. Because it is the best provider of economic security to women, children, and even men [...] And because nothing comes close to the family in giving children a secure and stable childhood.[2]

Ancient Israel had an enormous interest in not only honoring God but also in preserving the stability and harmony within the community, and therefore they took adultery very seriously. That leads us to our examination of a piece of Torah legislation found in Numbers 5:11-31, which raises a lot of questions surrounding the treatment of women in the Bible. This peculiar passage describes how to conduct a ritual trial if a man suspects that his wife committed adultery. As Richard Davidson remarks, "Feminists have often cited this legislation as their coup de grace proving the sexist nature of the OT."[3] Feminists complain that this passage promotes forcing a woman to endure a humiliating trial simply to satisfy the jealous rage of her husband, who was triggered by his baseless suspicions. How do we understand this difficult passage?

To give a summary, these laws are dealing with two possible situations: 1) a husband suspects his wife of being unfaithful after she had committed adultery (Numbers 5:12-14a); 2) a husband suspects his wife of being unfaithful even though she had *not* committed adultery (Numbers 5:14b). In either case, the husband can bring his wife before the Levitical priest to accuse her (Numbers 5:15).

It is vital not to lose sight of the fact, as we go along, that the husband has no proof of his wife's unfaithfulness in either situation.

---

2 Dennis Prager, *The Rational Bible: Exodus* (Washington, DC: Regnery, 2018)

3 Richard M. Davidson, *Flame of Yahweh: Sexuality in the Old Testament* (Peabody, MA: Hendrickson Publishers, 2007), p. 353

Usually, when it comes to charges of adultery, two witnesses are required in order to legally prosecute (Deuteronomy 17:6-7). This is a unique situation whereby the only basis for the "trial" is the husband's suspicion. Because there are no witnesses to the alleged adultery, the death penalty, which is the prescribed punishment for such a crime, cannot be carried out.

Since the husband's suspicion alone is not enough to legally prove adultery, it is beyond the jurisdiction of the human court to make a ruling. Therefore, the matter is put into God's hands, who will Himself either vindicate the woman if she is innocent or enact judgment on the woman if she is guilty. Before undergoing this ritual trial, the woman is required to take an oath, declaring that she accepts God's ruling (Numbers 5:19-24). Then she is required to drink the "water of bitterness"—a mixture of water with some dust from the floor of the tabernacle and parchment fragments (Numbers 5:17, 23-24). If she is innocent, the water has no effect on her. However, if she is guilty, the water causes her thigh to "fall away" and her body to "swell." The water causes "bitter pain" and then passes into her bowels and makes her abdomen swell (Numbers 5:21-22, 27).

While this passage might appear problematic on the surface, when we take a closer look, like other laws in the Torah, this ritual is actually designed for the protection of women. Concerning the feminist criticisms of this legislation, renowned scholar Jacob Milgrom writes, "Ironically, feminists have chosen the worst possible witness." He goes on to declare that the accused woman's public ordeal "was meant not to humiliate her but to protect her, not to punish her but to defend her."[4] Milgrom's conclusion will become clear as we

---

4   Jacob Milgrom, "A Husband's Pride, A Mob's Prejudice: The Public Ordeal Undergone by a Suspected Adulteress in Numbers 5 Was Meant Not to Humiliate Her but to Protect

address each of the common feminist objections concerning this legislation.

One objection often raised is that the basis for this ritual trial is unjust—a man dragging his wife to the priest and then forcing her to undergo a "humiliating" ritual. Why? Because the man has paranoid suspicions that his wife is cheating on him? That's so sexist! But let's think this through.

First, it should be noted that a husband was not *required* to invoke this law.[5] Nevertheless, if he suspected his wife of infidelity, this was one of the legal means that the Torah offered to resolve the issue. For those who find such a thing objectionable, I would ask, what should be the alternative? Should unresolved suspicions of adultery be left alone to fester within the marriage, evolving into distrust and resentment? If we leave things unresolved, what would stop the man from assuming the worst and taking matters into his own hands, which could potentially put the woman in a dangerous position?

In reality, not having this law in place could leave the door open for abuse. In stark contrast to other ancient Near Eastern law codes, which allowed for husbands to physically harm their wives as punishment,[6] the ritual trial of Numbers 5 serves to protect the woman from

---

Her," *Bible Review* 12.4 (1996): 21

5   See Timothy R. Ashley, *The Book of Numbers: The New International Commentary on the Old Testament* (Grand Rapids, MI: Wm. B. Eerdmans Publishing Co., 1993): "The verbal tenses in the main verbs in the passage are all either imperfects or perfects consecutive. These tenses may denote potential action; they need not denote a mandated action." (p. 126, fn 36)

6   See "The Middle Assyrian Laws (A59)," translated by Martha Roth, *Law Collections from Mesopotamia and Asia Minor* (Atlanta, GA: Society of Biblical Literature, 1995): "In addition to the punishments for [a man's wife] that are [written] on the tablet, a man may [whip] his wife, pluck out her hair, mutilate her ears, or strike her, with impunity." (pp. 175-176)

potential violence on the part of her jealous husband. It also prevented men from indiscriminately accusing their wives of adultery. If the husband had suspicions, his only recourse for resolving them was to defer to God through priestly mediation.

In addition to protecting the woman in this scenario, this legislation gave the family an opportunity to clear her name if she is innocent. Indeed, it's unreasonable to assume that the husband is just paranoid. As Victor H. Matthews points out, the more likely situation is that "there have been accusations made to him privately and rumor (represented by the statement in vv. 12-13) is beginning to bring public shame on his household."[7] So it's more likely that the husband's suspicions are aroused due to private accusations against his wife and rumors circling within the community. The husband can then choose to bring his wife before a third-party mediator—that is, the Levitical priest—in order to resolve the matter, clear his wife's name if she is innocent, and restore peace within the family and community.

Furthermore, if she were innocent, the woman would likely *want* to go through the trial. It is an opportunity to clear her name of malicious rumors. The "water of bitterness" itself is harmless—it's just dusty water. She simply pledges an oath of innocence and drinks it, and then when nothing happens, she's fully exonerated. The only reason she would have to be concerned is if she's guilty, in which case God will supernaturally give a sign that serves as her judgment.

This law goes even further to extend mercy to the woman *even if she is guilty*. Adultery is punishable by death (Leviticus 20:10), yet the woman proven guilty in Numbers 5 is not to be condemned to capital punishment. The sentencing is completely taken out of human hands.

---

7   Matthews, Levinson, and Frymer-Kensky, *Gender and Law in the Hebrew Bible* (Sheffield Academic Press, 1998), pp. 103-104

Neither the husband nor the community has a right to impose additional legal penalties. As Milgrom writes:

> [The trial] provides the priestly legislator with an accepted practice by which he could remove the sentencing and punishing of an unapprehended adulteress from human hands and thereby guarantee that she would not be put to death.[8]

Now let's consider another objection. Feminists and other critics have often referred to this ritual trial as a "trial by ordeal." A trial by ordeal was a judicial practice whereby a verdict was reached via subjecting the accused to a painful or dangerous test. Wendy Alsup gives a great summary:

> The Salem witch trials in colonial Massachusetts made Trial by Ordeal famous. Such trials have a long history in many cultures throughout the world. There were various types of trials—trials by fire, trials by burning oil, trials by hot water, trials by cold water, trials by drinking acid, and trials by combat. Most medieval Trials by Ordeal had a common theme, that the gods would protect an innocent person from being harmed. Throw someone tied up into a cold river, and if he was innocent, he'd miraculously float to the top. Force a woman to walk across hot coals, and if she was not burned (or her burns healed quickly), she was innocent of the accusations against her. Religious leaders believed the miraculous inter-

---

8   Jacob Milgrom, "A Husband's Pride, A Mob's Prejudice: The Public Ordeal Undergone by a Suspected Adulteress in Numbers 5 Was Meant Not to Humiliate Her but to Protect Her," *Bible Review* 12.4 (1996): 21

vention of the gods would keep a person safe in a situation meant to harm them. That's how most ancient trials by ordeal worked.[9]

While the situation in Numbers 5 can technically be classified as a trial by ordeal, such a classification is somewhat misleading. The trial in Numbers 5 cannot really be compared to other trials by ordeal since there is one major difference: the trial of Numbers 5 presumes innocence until guilt is proven. Davidson highlights this difference by comparing the biblical legislation to a parallel law in another ancient Near Eastern law code known as the Code of Hammurabi. In this Mesopotamian counterpart to the biblical law, the woman was thrown into a sacred river whereby her innocence was established if she survived.[10] The ritual trial outlined in the biblical legislation "required a miracle in order to condemn the woman," whereas the Code of Hammurabi's legislation "required a miracle in order for the woman to be regarded as innocent."[11]

Indeed, other trials by ordeal required the accused to survive something inherently dangerous in order to prove their innocence. The trial of Numbers 5, however, is naturally harmless. The "water of bitterness" that the suspected adulteress had to drink probably didn't

---

9   Wendy Alsup, *Practical Theology for Women.* "Is Numbers 5 Good for Women?" www. theologyforwomen.com. Accessed 9/16/19

10   See "Laws of Hammurabi (132)," translated by Martha Roth, *Law Collections from Mesopotamia and Asia Minor* (Atlanta, GA: Society of Biblical Literature, 1995): "If a man's wife should have a finger pointed against her in accusation involving another male, although she has not been seized lying with another male, she shall submit to the divine River Ordeal for her husband." (p. 106)

11   Richard M. Davidson, *Flame of Yahweh: Sexuality in the Old Testament* (Peabody, MA: Hendrickson Publishers, 2007), p. 352-353

taste very good, but the concoction in itself didn't do anything to hurt the woman. If she was innocent, she had nothing to worry about—and again, she likely would *want* to go through the trial if it meant being exonerated. If she were guilty, she would deserve punishment, as would a man found guilty of adultery. The only way that harm could come upon the woman was by a supernatural miracle if she was guilty.

Another criticism feminists raise is that this text is silent about what a woman is to do if she suspects *her husband* of unfaithfulness. Wouldn't this be an example of legal inequality since it appears that the Torah provides no recourse for women in such a situation? Well, Copan suggests that the text actually allows for the wife to call for this ritual trial. He argues that when we consider the context, we have "every reason to think that this law applied to men as well," and then he highlights the fact that the legislation before and after this passage concerns both men and women (Numbers 5:2; 5:6; 6:2).[12] Maybe Copan has a point. In either case, we do know that the Torah—at least how it was interpreted by Jews in the first century—permitted women to divorce their husbands, which would give the woman some recourse if she found herself in a situation wherein her husband had been unfaithful. On the basis of historical evidence from Elephantine and Philo, Sigal argues that the right to pursue a divorce was accorded to women as well as to men in the first century.[13] Yeshua likewise mentions the woman's ability to divorce her husband in Mark 10:12.

---

12 Paul Copan, *Is God a Moral Monster?: Making Sense of the Old Testament God* (Grand Rapids, MI: Baker Publishing Group, 2011), p. 105

13 Phillip Sigal, *The Halakhah of Jesus of Nazareth According to the Gospel of Matthew* (Atlanta, GA: Society of Biblical Literature, 2007): "If it is the woman who has the freedom of choice, as Philo interprets Deut 22:19 (and, one might add, Deut 22:29), it would appear that she had a prerabbinic right to divorce her husband. We have seen this at Elephantine, and it was customary throughout the GrecoRoman world. But by the

Nevertheless, the ritual trial of Numbers 5 clearly demonstrates the value and personhood of women. The Torah declares that a jealous husband's word is not enough to convict a woman of a crime. Women, just like me, deserve due process and the presumption of innocence. And if she is innocent, the ritual trial guarantees her complete exoneration.

Does the Torah Sanction Abortion?

This passage in Numbers raises another objection to biblical ethics regarding abortion. Some skeptics, and even liberal so-called Christians, will insist that the woman in this passage is pregnant and that the concoction she drinks causes her to miscarry. In other words, they say that the priest essentially performs an abortion on the woman through having her drink the waters of bitterness. These skeptics believe that the liquid somehow causes the fetus to discharge from the woman's womb. Based on these assumptions, some will argue that the Bible sanctions abortion.

Unfortunately, one English translation is incredibly misleading, lending support to this objection. In the oath that the woman has to agree to, the priest says the following:

> "The Lord make you a curse and an oath among your people
> by the Lord's making your thigh waste away and your abdo-
> men swell; and this water that brings a curse shall go into your
> stomach, and make your abdomen swell and your thigh waste

time Josephus writes, with rabbinic halakhah in the dominant position, he says this is contrary to halakhah. It appears, as well, from references in the Palestinian Talmud that Philo's statement implying a woman may freely choose to divorce her husband was the earlier halakhah. Mark 10:12 is testimony to this halakhic alternative." (p. 134)

away." And the woman shall say, "Amen. Amen." (Numbers 5:21-22, NASB)

But this is what the NIV says:

"May the Lord cause you to become a curse among your people when he makes your womb miscarry and your abdomen swell. May this water that brings a curse enter your body so that your abdomen swells or your womb miscarries." Then the woman is to say, "Amen. So be it." (Numbers 5:21-22, NIV)

The Hebrew word translated "miscarry" in the NIV is *naphal*, which means to fall. The word "womb" is *yarek*, which means thigh or side. The NIV translation is unique among all other major English translations in this regard. It's the only translation that indicates a miscarriage occurring here, which is a clear mistranslation. All other English translations say "thigh fall away," "thigh rot," etc. Moreover, neither the Septuagint's rendering of this verse[14] nor Josephus' description of the curse (Antiquities of the Jews 3.11.6) indicates a miscarriage. None of the later rabbinic literature on this passage suggests that the curse includes miscarriage.[15] The idea rests solely on the NIV translation.

---

14   See Pietersma & Write, *A New English Translation of the Septuagint* (Oxford University Press, 2007): "And this water that brings the curse shall enter your belly, to swell the belly and make your thigh fall to pieces" (Numbers 5:22, LXX).

15   Maimonides suggested that the exact same curse will fall upon the adulterer. Men obviously have no womb and thus cannot miscarry, which entails that this curse does not indicate miscarriage. See Maimonides, *Mishneh Torah, Sefer Nashim*: "The same phenomena, the swelling of the belly and the rupture of the thigh, will also occur to

But what exactly *does* this curse entail? Well, the language used of the body swelling and the thigh rotting is ambiguous. However, scholars have offered a few suggestions. Roy Gane observes that the word for thigh "apparently connotes reproductive organs," and thus, the curse of the thigh wasting away "can be taken to imply sterility and may refer to a prolapsed uterus."[16] Timothy Ashley offers similar thoughts:

> The rendering of the second punishment has been much debated. Most modern English translations agree on a rendering something like "a fallen thigh and a swollen belly" [...] Since the blessing connected with the innocent woman is the ability to bear children, most commentators connect the curse with the stoppage of child-bearing. The word thigh (yarek), in addition to its literal meaning of the upper part of the leg, seems to be used euphemistically of the seat of procreative power in men, due perhaps to the thigh's proximity to the sexual organs. This passage is the only place where such a usage is found for a female. A fallen thigh, therefore, seems to indicate the falling or atrophying of the sexual organ so as to make childbearing impossible.[17]

There seems to be a consensus among scholars that, whatever the physical manifestation this curse takes, the result is barrenness. And this seems to be clearly indicated in the text itself since the woman

---

him." (Sotah 3:17)

16   Roy Gane, *The NIV Application Commentary: Leviticus, Numbers* (Grand Rapids, MI: Zondervan, 2004), p. 523

17   Timothy R. Ashley, *The Book of Numbers: The New International Commentary on the Old Testament* (Grand Rapids, MI: Wm. B. Eerdmans Publishing Co., 1993), p. 132

is reassured that she will continue to be able to bear children if she is innocent (Numbers 5:28).

In either case, nothing in the text even hints that a fetus is killed as part of this curse. A couple of reasons can be given in support of this conclusion. First, nowhere in the text is there any indication that the woman is even pregnant. That idea is simply read into the text by skeptics, but it's an unwarranted assumption. This fact alone is enough to dismiss the idea that this passage is describing an abortion. Second, nothing inherent in the "waters of bitterness" would affect the woman's body or cause a miscarriage, and this is proven by the fact that it would not affect her if she is innocent.

In conclusion, far from being an example of the mistreatment of women, Numbers 5:11-31 demonstrates God's utmost care for the protection of women. It protected women from the unpredictable reaction of a jealous husband by requiring priestly mediation. The law demonstrates that a woman's life and reputation cannot be destroyed on the basis of male accusations, but that she deserves due process and fairness. The law also provided a way to resolve suspicions within the marriage that could destroy a family if left unresolved. It provided a way for a woman to clear her name and put to rest malicious rumors within the community. It even extends mercy to a woman who is guilty of adultery by not demanding she be put to death or be subjected to any other additional penalties imposed by the human court. Moreover, contrary to the claims of some skeptics, nothing in the passage gives even the slightest hint of an endorsement of abortion. Once again, even in this difficult passage, Scripture reminds us of the wisdom, justice, and mercy of God in providing care and protection for women.

CHAPTER 4
UNDERSTANDING THE TEST FOR VIRGINITY

Feminist critics often cite the biblical legislation found in Deuteronomy 22:13-21 as proof of the Bible's sexism. According to feminists, the Bible teaches that "used brides deserve death."[1] That is to say, the Torah demands capital punishment for women who are discovered not to be virgins at the time they got married. But what does the Bible actually say?

The legislation found in Deuteronomy 22:13-21, commonly referred to as "the Case of the Slandered Bride," presents a hypothetical scenario in which a man finds himself dissatisfied with his new wife after their wedding night. So what does he do? He tries to get out of the marriage and forsake his responsibility toward his new wife by accusing her of not being a virgin when he married her (22:14). In this scenario, the parents of the young bride could testify on her behalf and provide evidence of her virginity to exonerate her (22:15); the husband would then be punished and fined for disgracing his wife and her family through his false accusation. However, if the husband's accusation was proved to be true, the young woman would be executed.

The Value of Virginity

This passage raises a lot of questions. However, before we get into the specifics, we must investigate the high value placed on virginity in the Scripture.

---

1   Valerie Tarico, "Owned: Slaves, Women, Children, and Livestock," *Women v. Religion: The Case Against Faith* (Durham, NC: Pitchstone Publishing, 2018), p. 112

According to the Bible, the only appropriate context for sex is marriage. Thus, premarital sex is completely prohibited. In fact, if a man seduces a virgin, the Torah demands he take responsibility and marry her—unless she and her family refuse (Exodus 22:15-16). Since sex is a sacred act to be enjoyed only within marriage, premarital virginity is extolled.

Feminists complain that the biblical virtue of premarital virginity is an expression of patriarchal oppression of women, which treats a woman's sexuality as the property of men.[2] However, this biblical virtue applies not only to women but also to men, so it cannot be a form of sexism.[3] Moreover, premarital sex is not merely a sin against one's spouse but a sin against God Himself. This entails that premarital sex is not simply a "property crime" against the husband. Atheists and others who reject biblical ethics will certainly consider premarital sex to be an imaginary crime made up by the ancient biblical authors. But we (who know the Bible contains God's revelation) understand the issue of remaining a virgin until marriage to be deeply rooted in theological truths about God and His relationship with mankind. Let's look at God's establishment of marriage at creation:

---

2   See Lauri Weissman, "Half Human: How Jewish Law Justifies the Exclusion and Exploitation of Women," *Ibid*: "The Israelite tribal society, like nearly all Bronze Age civilizations and a tragic percentage since, treats female sexuality as a male possession and characterizes violation of a woman as a property crime against the woman's owner, the man with legal claim over her reproductive capacity." (pp. 60-61)

3   See Tim Hegg, *Studies in the Torah: Deuteronomy* (Tacoma, WA: TorahResource, 2016): "Our Torah text makes it clear that God's intention is that a woman be a virgin when she marries. For a woman to remain a virgin until she marries means that men must also honor God's standards." (p. 154)

> Therefore a man shall leave his father and his mother and hold fast to his wife, and they shall become one flesh. (Genesis 2:24)

God's design for marriage involves several things: first, man is to "leave" all other previous family commitments in order to establish a new *exclusive* relationship with his wife. Second, husband and wife are to "hold fast" to each other—that is, they enter a committed, covenant relationship. Third, they are to "become one flesh." In other words, husband and wife are to have a deep and profound intimacy in their exclusive relationship as an expression of their one-flesh union.

According to the biblical view, therefore, sex has a purpose more profound than mere physical pleasure. Sex is much more than "the rubbing together of pieces of gut, followed by the spasmodic secretion of a little bit of slime."[4] Interestingly, humans, including nonreligious people, generally agree with the notion that sex matters in a deep way, which can be seen in secular society's own restrictions on sex. Explicit public sex, for example, is illegal. Society generally regards sex as a private and intimate activity. Sex is also restricted regarding close relatives, minors, non-consenting adults, etc. Why? Because everyone agrees that sex is important, intimate, and not something to be casually thrown away or taken from someone.[5] Thus, the fact that the Bible gives restrictions on sexual activity isn't *that* strange of an idea.

The Bible teaches that sex is a powerful expression of intimacy enjoyed within a covenant of love. The biblical authors often use marriage as a metaphor to describe God's relationship with His people. Just like marriage between man and wife, the relationship between God

---

4   Marcus Aurelius, *Meditations 6.13*, quoted in Alexander R. Pruss, *One Body: An Essay in Christian Sexual Ethics* (Notre Dame, IN: Notre Dame Press, 2013), p. 66

5   For a great argument on the objective meaningfulness of sexuality, see Ibid., esp. pp. 61-88

and His people is to be exclusive, committed, and intimate. We are commanded not to have any other gods but to worship only the Lord (e.g., Exodus 34:14). This is why, throughout the prophets, Israel's idolatry is often compared to adultery. God's commandments and expectations for His people are not arbitrary religious rules. In addition to protecting our human relationships, they teach us about God, His character, and how we relate to Him. Thus, it is no surprise that God's laws governing the marriage relationship between husband and wife give us a picture of what our relationship with the Lord is supposed to look like.

One of the ways that the Bible underscores the importance of sexual exclusivity in the marriage relationship is by emphasizing the value of premarital virginity. Sex is sacred, and the sexual union is an exclusive act of intimacy to be enjoyed only within the boundaries of a committed covenant relationship between husband and wife. Engaging in this sacred act outside of the boundaries of marriage by having premarital sex profanes the sacredness of the sexual union.

How does premarital sex profane the sacredness of marital sex? Think of sex as a precious gift. Giving this gift away to people who aren't your spouse decreases the unique significance of the gift. It sacrifices an aspect of the full expression of marital love for the sake of temporary pleasure. It defrauds your future spouse of the exclusive intimacy God intends in marriage. Premarital sex brings harm not only upon you and your future spouse but also upon the partner(s) with whom you have sex: it robs from them an aspect of the exclusivity and unique significance of their own full expression of intimacy in their future marriage.

In addition, God knows that premarital sex could potentially be harmful on a practical level. According to a major study of college-aged women in America, "[H]ookup behavior during college was positively correlated with experiencing clinically significant depression symptoms."[6] Another study regarding teenagers concluded that "teenagers who engage in casual sex are more likely to suffer from depression than their peers who don't engage in casual sex [...] Given that teens who practiced celibacy were rated lowest for clinical depression and depressive symptoms on the charts, promiscuity may be symptomatic of depression."[7]

A big reason that casual sex often relates to depression is that sex was intended to occur only within the boundaries of covenant marriage wherein each spouse feels cherished and protected. Sex outside of that context degrades one's human dignity. Moreover, spouses have often had to work through distrust, jealousy, and insecurity in their marriage due to one or both of them engaging in sexual intimacy with other people before they married each other. Those marital issues can be resolved by the grace of God, but this simple fact of life once again underscores why the Bible speaks to these important issues.

Given the value placed upon marriage and sex, the family had a responsibility to guard the purity of Israelite daughters/sisters (e.g., Genesis 34:13-31), hence why the parents of the bride get involved in testifying on behalf of their daughter in Deuteronomy 22:13-21. Modern feminists often look down upon these family values as oppressive, but women in the ancient world didn't think that at all. As we shall discover, ancient women benefited greatly and were protected because of these values.

---

6   Robyn L. Fielder et al., "Sexual Hookups and Abverse Health Outcomes: A Longitudinal Study of First-Year College Women," *The Journal of Sex Research* vol. 51 (2014), quoted in Dennis Prager, *The Rational Bible: Exodus* (Washington, DC: Regnery, 2018)

7   Ugo Uche, "A Link Between Sexual Promiscuity and Depression in Teens," *Psychology Today*, quoted in Ibid.

In Defense of the Bride

Back to our passage in question, several considerations are important to keep in mind as we interpret this legislation. The first thing to point out is that these laws actually protected the young woman by presuming her innocence and requiring due process. Without this legislation, a man could slander his new wife, ruin her reputation in the community, and divorce her without warrant, destroying her life. But with this legislation, a falsely accused bride could be fully exonerated and repair her reputation that was damaged due to malicious lies about her moral integrity.

What is especially interesting about the hypothetical scenario outlined in Deuteronomy 22:13-21 is that we often assume the husband is the plaintiff in this case. However, the Torah turns the situation around on the husband, making him the defendant! The legislation begins on the premise that the husband decides he "hates" his new wife and wants out of the marriage (22:13), so he sets out to slander her among the community, publically charging her with not being a virgin on their wedding night (22:14). Thus, the young bride's parents "initiate the proceedings to have their daughter's sullied reputation cleared"[8] (22:15). The bride's father then accuses *the husband* of being unfaithful to his daughter by his dishonest attempt to abandon his marital commitments (22:16). Evidence is then presented that clears the bride and convicts the husband (22:17). The evidence provided by the young bride's family "trumps the verbal accusations of a treacherous husband."[9] Once the young woman's innocence is established, the elders of the community take the man and punish him, which

8   Daniel Block, *The NIV Application Commentary: Deuteronomy* (Grand Rapids, MI: Zondervan, 2012), p. 522

9   Ibid., p. 523

consisted of public flogging[10] in addition to a fine of one hundred shekels of silver (22:18-19). Thus, this law ultimately served to deter men from making such serious and baseless allegations against their wives.

In addition to being flogged and fined, the man is prohibited from ever divorcing his wife. His shameful behavior "prevented the man from achieving in the end what he had set out to do in the first place."[11] Modern readers might find that troubling. If the man hates his wife and he's a proven liar, wouldn't it be better for them just to get divorced? But this prescription "forces [the husband] to guarantee her economic well-being for life."[12] Daniel Block also makes the following observation:

> [T]his requirement aims for a rehabilitative outcome. Because the matter is resolved in a public court of law, the people in the community become guarantors of the man's good behavior.[13]

Contrary to the complaints of critics, the Torah is clearly concerned about a woman's welfare, including her name and reputation. The reason the Torah gives for the husband's punishment is that he "brought a bad name upon a virgin of Israel" (Deuteronomy 22:19). Indeed, in the community governed by Torah, men could not treat

---

10 See Peter C. Craigie, *The New International Commentary on the Old Testament: Deuteronomy* (Grand Rapids, MI: William B. Eerdmans Publishing Company, 1976): "The Hebrew word (*yisser*) implies corporal punishment, such as a flogging." (p. 293)

11 Ibid.

12 Daniel Block, "You Shall Not Covet Your Neighbor's Wife: A Study in Deuteronomic Domestic Ideology," *Journal of the Evangelical Theological Society*; Vol. 53 (2010), p. 467

13 Daniel Block, *The NIV Application Commentary: Deuteronomy* (Grand Rapids, MI: Zondervan, 2012), p. 523

women like property or second-class citizens. They couldn't falsely accuse women and expect to get away with it. The Torah demands that God's people be committed to protecting and honoring women.

Regarding the specific evidence that the parents provided to exonerate the young woman, the passage speaks of a "cloth" that was presented before the elders of the city. According to most scholars, this cloth refers to a garment placed on the marriage bed, which would contain blood from the breaking of the young woman's hymen during initial sexual intercourse.[14] This cloth was then given to the bride's family to be safely stored as "evidence," indicating that she was a virgin on the wedding night.

Many modern readers are troubled by this common ancient Near Eastern practice and understandably question its reliability. For instance, what if the young woman was a virgin, but she simply didn't bleed her first time having sex? Or what if her hymen had broken from a non-sexual activity before the wedding night? Isn't this pretty shaky evidence upon which to base a death sentence, putting the woman at an extreme legal disadvantage?

A few considerations can be made in response to the objection that the bride is at a disadvantage in this case: first, the assumption that the evidence presented by the bride's parents was limited to only this cloth is unreasonable. The testimony of the bride's family, in addition to the lack of actual evidence provided by the husband, likewise weighed in favor of the bride.

---

14   See Peter C. Craigie, *The New International Commentary on the Old Testament: Deuteronomy* (Grand Rapids, MI: William B. Eerdmans Publishing Company, 1976: "The evidence consisted of his daughter's tokens of virginity; a token would have been a sheet or garment marked with blood, coming from the marriage chamber of the daughter on the wedding night. The blood would be evidence that, at the time of the consummation of the marriage, the young woman had been a virgin." (p. 292-293)

Second, the matter was to be addressed publically before the community elders, which provided an additional layer of protection for the bride as well as a deterrent to a husband raising baseless allegations. The elders had a responsibility and an interest in protecting the members of the community, which would have included not only appropriately dealing with promiscuity but also preventing the unjust sentencing of an innocent woman. Out of a fear of the Lord, they would have taken special care not to risk condemning the innocent.

Third, as Frymer-Kensky observes, the blood-stained cloth could easily be faked in order to establish the bride's innocence.[15] Thus, far from putting the bride at a legal disadvantage, the fact that such evidence is admissible in the court essentially guarantees that she would be exonerated.

What If the Accusations Are True?

While this legislation is concerned primarily with defending the young bride against false charges, a severe punishment is handed down if the husband's accusations prove to be true. If the young bride and her family lied about her virginity, thereby deceiving her husband, she was to be executed (22:20-21). Now, some might object that this

---

15   See Tikva Frymer-Kensky, *Studies in Bible and Feminist Criticism* (Philadelphia, PA: The Jewish Publication Society, 2006): "There is good reason to suspect that this law was not expected to be followed. According to the procedure laid out in Deuteronomy 22:13–4, after the accusation, the case was brought before the elders at the gate, and the parents of the girl produced the sheet to prove that she was a virgin; once they did this, the man was flogged, fined, and lost his rights to divorce her in the future. Since the parents had plenty of time to find blood for the sheets, it is unlikely that a bridegroom would make such a charge; if he disliked the girl he could divorce her. If nevertheless made such a charge, she and her family would have to be very ignorant not to fake the blood." (p. 243)

punishment for the woman's premarital sexual activity is unreasonably harsh. A few points are worthy of consideration here.

First, the specific crime for which the bride is executed does not seem to be the act of premarital sex itself but that she *deceived* her husband about such an important matter.[16] We know from other passages in which premarital sex is explicitly addressed that the Torah does not consider the act to be a crime punishable by death (Exodus 22:16-17; Deuteronomy 22:28-29). Thus, the difference with this law is the deceit on the part of the young woman. As Davidson observes:

> The punishment for this illicit premarital sexual activity is considerably more strict than a clear case of consensual premarital sex on the part of an unmarried, unbetrothed girl: it is equivalent to that of adultery by a married or betrothed woman. Apparently what makes the punishment equivalent to that of adultery even if the sexual intercourse took place before betrothal is that the girl concealed from her husband her premarital sexual activity, and in such case it was to be assumed that it was illicit sex after betrothal. The serious, but not capital, offense of premarital sex thus becomes a capital offense because of the element of deceit and false pretense to premarital chastity: she has entered into marriage without acknowledging her prior loss of virginity.[17]

---

16   See John Walton, Victor Matthews, & Mark Chavalas, *The IVP Bible Background Commentary: Old Testament* (Downers Grove, IL: IVP Academic): "Virginity prior to marriage was prized as a means of insuring that one's children and heirs were actually one's own. The integrity of the woman's household was based on her being able to show proof of her virginity." (p. 295)

17   Richard M. Davidson, *Flame of Yahweh: Sexuality in the Old Testament* (Peabody, MA: Hendrickson Publishers, 2007), p. 358

Second, to put it simply, God takes sin seriously. Some sins warrant the death penalty according to the Bible, and this is one of them. However, lest feminists complain about the supposed biblical inequality in this regard, it should be noted that this particular sin is not the only one worthy of capital punishment in the Torah. The Torah prescribes the death penalty for many other transgressions, such as idolatry, breaking the Sabbath, murder, homosexual acts, etc., and men are just as capable as women of committing such capital crimes. The purpose of instituting the death penalty was primarily to deter God's people from engaging in destructive sins as well as to remove from the community unrepentant sinners who have contempt for God and the welfare of their fellow man. Israel vowed to obey God's laws. If anyone wanted to experience the blessings and benefits of living in this holy nation, they had to abide by the terms of the covenant that they agreed to. Copan puts it well:

> Israel had bound herself to Yahweh, who had made a covenant with Israel—like a husband to a wife. The people of Israel themselves had vowed that they were God's and that they would keep his covenant (Exod. 24:3). They had willingly submitted to God's (theocratic) rule [...] Of course, those not wanting to embrace Israel's God or obey his requirements were free to leave Israel and live in another nation. This was the obvious, preferable alternative. It was spiritually healthier for Israel and safer for theocracy opposers. Any remaining in the land were to respect the covenant and the laws that went with it.[18]

18 Paul Copan, *Is God a Moral Monster?: Making Sense of the Old Testament God* (Grand Rapids, MI: Baker Publishing Group, 2011), p. 129

Third, throughout history, there is not a single record of a woman ever being sentenced to death in accordance with this biblical legislation. We don't know if such a scenario, as described in Deuteronomy 22:13-21, has ever even happened in reality. Some scholars, like Frymer-Kensky, suggest that "there is good reason to suspect that this law was not expected to be followed"[19] due to the unlikelihood that the husband would pursue such charges in light of the fact that he would most certainly lose the lawsuit. In other words, the legislation essentially sets the husband up to fail, and therefore it served primarily as a deterrent to making slanderous accusations against "a virgin of Israel" (Deuteronomy 22:19).

Fourth, if we assume that this legislation was expected to be followed, this entire situation is completely avoidable in a number of ways. For instance, most importantly, men and women could simply remain virgins until marriage. That is obviously the ideal situation. Moreover, a husband could love his wife and therefore not slander her. That would avoid the need for the wife's parents to initiate court proceedings to clear their daughter's name of false accusations. If the young woman did have premarital sex with another man, another way to avoid this scenario would be for her to disclose this information to her potential future husband. The man could then choose whether or not to forgive her and marry her anyway. But if he doesn't marry her, premarital sex itself does not warrant the death penalty. Thus, she would be free to go about her life and perhaps marry someone else who would be willing to overlook her past.

In conclusion, while premarital sex is a serious sin, the main sins condemned in the hypothetical scenario outlined in Deuteron-

---

19   Tikva Frymer-Kensky, *Studies in Bible and Feminist Criticism* (Philadelphia, PA: The Jewish Publication Society, 2006), p. 243

omy 22:13-21 are slander and deception. This legislation is designed to protect women and provide a means for them to clear their name if their husbands slander them. As we saw, this law does not allow the possibility of innocent women to be executed. However, if the husband's accusations are proven true in a court of law, the woman is to be executed. Again, she isn't sentenced to death simply because she wasn't a virgin when she got married, but because, like with adultery, there was an element of deceit in her actions. This is not unlike other capital crimes throughout the Bible that both men and women are capable of committing. Finally, it's likely the laws outlined in Deuteronomy 22:13-21 have never actually been enforced in reality but served simply as a deterrent against slander and promiscuity in the community.

CHAPTER 5
UNDERSTANDING THE BIBLE'S PASSAGES ABOUT RAPE

"I thought that training for the Olympics would be the hardest thing I would ever have to do," former Olympic gymnast Jordyn Wieber said. "But the hardest thing I've ever had to do is process that I am a victim of Larry Nassar."[1] Wieber made this powerful comment during the sentencing hearing of Larry Nassar, a former USA Gymnastics national team doctor who sexually assaulted hundreds of young female athletes during their medical appointments. Many other survivors testified, gave compelling and moving statements, and called for the maximum punishment allowable for their abuser. Nassar was sentenced to 40-175 years in prison,[2] which is nothing compared to the immense pain and trauma he had inflicted upon his victims. But what if instead of going to prison, Nassar was sentenced to having to marry his victims? That is what feminist critics say the Torah requires—that rapists marry their victims.[3]

---

1   Morgan Brinlee, *Bustle*. "Quotes From Larry Nassar's Abuse Victims That Will Just Crush You." www.bustle.com. Accessed 9/25/19

2   Ibid.

3   See Candace Gorham, "Guilt, Shame, and Psychological Pain," *Women v. Religion: The Case Against Faith—and for Freedom*. Karen L. Garst, ed. (Durham, NC: Pitchstone Publishing, 2018): "The Old Testament has uniquely disturbing stances on rape and sexual violence, how they are defined, and how they should be handled legally. For example, the laws in Deuteronomy 22 explain the various ways judgment could be passed on a rapist and his victim: death of the victim and the assailant, the death of the assailant only, or the marriage of the victim and the assailant—the determining factors being the location of the rape (city versus country) and the marital status of the woman." (pp. 36-37)

The basis for this objection is Deuteronomy 22:28-29, which states that if a man "seizes" a young virgin and has sex with her, he is to pay her father fifty shekels of silver[4] and marry her. He is also never allowed to divorce her. Feminists allege that this passage is clear proof that the Bible regards women as the property of men. According to feminists, the female victim in this passage is "sold" to the rapist who violently attacked and degraded her. How do we address this difficult objection?

The passage in question is preceded by legislation in Deuteronomy 22:25-27 that clearly addresses rape. According to verses 25-27, if a man "seizes" (*chazaq*) a woman in an open field, the Torah demands he be put to death. But the young woman is presumed innocent since nobody would have been able to hear her cries for help.[5] This passage uses a different Hebrew word for "seizes" than is used in verse 28. The verb *chazaq* has a basic meaning of "to be strong,"[6] and can refer "to the violent overpowering of another and, in the context of this text, clearly denotes rape."[7] The Bible, therefore, regards rape as a horrific and violent act comparable to murder: "For this case is like that of a man attacking and murdering his neighbor" (Deuteronomy 22:26). The woman in this scenario is portrayed as a victim worthy of justice, not the property of men. And unlike other ancient law codes like the Middle Assyrian Laws, which called for retaliatory rape upon

---

4   The biblical custom of the "bride-price" is addressed in the next chapter.

5   See Tim Hegg, *Studies in the Torah: Deuteronomy* (Tacoma, WA: TorahResource, 2016): "Where evidence of the woman crying out is impossible to ascertain, the woman is presumed innocent. The law gives precedence to the woman over the man in this case." (p. 155)

6   Ibid., p. 156

7   Katie McCoy, *BiblicalWoman.* "God is Not Silent About Rape." www.biblicalwoman.com. Accessed 9/25/19

an assailant's wife,[8] the Torah upholds the value and personhood of women by punishing only the rapist—legal penalties were not applied to innocent family members.

When we continue to verses 28-29, we discover that they seem to describe a different type of situation than that described in verses 25-27. While verses 25-27 certainly speak of rape, verses 28-29 speak of a young couple's consensual sexual encounter. This perspective can be demonstrated in a few ways. For instance, as already mentioned, the Hebrew word for "seizes," *taphas*, used here in verse 28, is different from the term used in the prior legislation dealing with forcible rape. While *taphas* does generally mean to "capture" or "seize," unlike *chazaq*, "[*taphas*] does not carry the same connotation of force."[9] In fact, when rape is depicted later in the Hebrew scriptures, *chazaq*, not *taphas*, is the word that is used (Judges 19:25; 2 Samuel 13:11, 14). If the biblical author intended to describe rape in verses 28-29, it's reasonable to think he would use *chazaq* as he does in verses 25-27, but he doesn't. In addition to not carrying the same connotation of violence as *chazaq*, the term *taphas* is also used in metaphors to speak of things like God "capturing the heart" of Israel (Ezekiel 14:5), which has led some scholars to interpret the use of *taphas* in this passage to imply that the man "seizes" the woman in an *emotional* sense.[10] This

---

8   See "The Middle Assyrian Laws (A55)," translated by Martha Roth, *Law Collections from Mesopotamia and Asia Minor* (Atlanta, GA: Society of Biblical Literature, 1995): "[T]he father of the maiden shall take the wife of the fornicator of the maiden and hand her over to be raped." (p. 175)

9   Katie McCoy, *CBMW*. "Did Old Testament Law Force a Woman to Marry Her Rapist?" www.cbmw.org. Accessed 9/25/19

10   See Lyn M. Bechtel, "What If Dinah Is Not Raped? (Genesis 34)," *JSOT*, Vol. 62 (1994): "In Deut. 22:28-29 a man finds and takes hold of or touches the heart of an unbounded young woman and lies with her. There is no cry for help from the woman and no violence on the part of the man. There is voluntary sexual intercourse between two unbounded

point is especially relevant when we consider this legislation in light of the parallel passage in Exodus:

> If a man seduces a virgin who is not betrothed and lies with her, he shall give the bride-price for her and make her his wife. If her father utterly refuses to give her to him, he shall pay money equal to the bride-price for virgins. (Exodus 22:16-17)

Deuteronomy 22:28-29 elaborates on this legislation in Exodus. Remarkably, rather than "seizes," the Exodus passage uses the verb *patah*, which means "seduces." In light of the parallel legislation in Exodus, then, it's likely that this section in Deuteronomy "does not deal with rape but with seduction."[11] In this scenario, the man persuades the young woman to engage in sex, and she consents. As Copan explains, "Even if there is some pressure from the man, the young woman is complicit; though initially pressured (seduced), she doesn't act against her will."[12] Also note that unlike the prior legislation in verses 25-27, verses 28-29 do not contain any mention of the woman crying for help. Thus, just like in Exodus, this legislation in Deuteronomy 22:28-29 is dealing with consensual sex between a young couple, not rape.

To be clear, I am certainly not suggesting that the woman in this scenario wasn't mistreated. From the Torah's perspective, the man still "violated" her (v. 29). Although she consented to sex, the man dishon-

---

people, but with no prospect of bonding and obligation. This too does not qualify as rape." (p. 25)

11 Tim Hegg, *Studies in the Torah: Deuteronomy* (Tacoma, WA: TorahResource, 2016), p. 156

12 Paul Copan, *Is God a Moral Monster?: Making Sense of the Old Testament God* (Grand Rapids, MI: Baker Publishing Group, 2011), p. 119

ored the young woman by persuading her to engage in sex without first giving her the dignity of marriage. Therefore, the Torah holds the man accountable for his behavior. According to both passages, two courses of action are given to address the couple's situation if, as Deuteronomy 22:28 says, "they are found" (caught having sex).

The first option is that the father gives permission to the man to marry his daughter.[13] In that scenario, the man pays the full bride-price of fifty shekels of silver to the father and is prohibited from ever divorcing the young woman. In the ancient world, the daughter in this situation would likely prefer this arrangement since it meant that her honor would be restored in marriage, and she would be taken care of. For the young woman, "this law ensured that she would not be objectified and discarded...In a culture where a woman's marriage equated to her financial provision, this law ensured her security."[14] In addition to providing security for the woman, Hegg suggests a pastoral element to the prohibition on divorce:

> This is an insightful restriction. Marriages which begin in fornication are often fraught with the inability of the couple to trust each other (for obvious reasons). Removing the possibility of divorce might strengthen a couple's need to build trust between each other.[15]

The second option is that the father exercises his legal right as the leader of the family to deny the man's request to marry his daughter

---

13   Even though the father is the one who makes the call, we shouldn't assume that the young woman had no say in the matter.

14   Katie McCoy, *CBMW*. "Did Old Testament Law Force a Woman to Marry Her Rapist?" www.cbmw.org. Accessed 9/25/19

15   Tim Hegg, *Studies in the Torah: Deuteronomy* (Tacoma, WA: TorahResource, 2016), p. 156

if he determines that such an arrangement wouldn't be in his daughter's best interests. In this case, the man is *still* required to pay the full bride-price as if the young woman were a virgin (Exodus 22:17). The bride-price being paid to the father doesn't entail that the Bible regards the daughter as the property of the father/husband, especially since it ultimately belonged to the daughter anyway, as we'll discuss in the next chapter. In either case, the man is held accountable for his actions, and the woman is provided for.

In conclusion, contrary to the claims of critics, the Bible does not sanction rape. Scripture depicts rape as a horrific and violent act comparable to murder and worthy of capital punishment. Female victims of rape are to be protected and cared for. The passage on which critics base their claim that the Bible requires victims to marry their rapists is actually not talking about rape at all. Several nuances (the use of *taphas* instead of *chazaq*; the fact that there is no mention of the woman crying for help; the consideration of the parallel passage in Exodus) indicate that Deuteronomy 22:28-29 describes a consensual sexual encounter in which the man persuades the young woman to have sex outside of marriage. In such a case, the law for the couple to get married is designed ultimately to provide protection and security for the woman and additionally to hold the man accountable for his actions, thus upholding the dignity and personhood of the woman. When it comes to women, men are not allowed to "love 'em and leave 'em," according to the Torah. Women aren't mere objects to be used, abused, and thrown away. Indeed, far from reflecting the character of some misogynistic deity who viewed women as inferior to men, God's laws once again demonstrate His love and concern for women—that they are worthy of honor, dignity, and protection.

CHAPTER 6
DOES GOD VIEW WOMEN AS INFERIOR TO MEN?

A persistent feminist criticism of the Bible is that it portrays women as inferior to men. As feminist author Valerie Tarico puts it, "In most of the Bible's texts, women are literally possessions of men, as are livestock, children, and slaves."[1] This accusation is intended to call into question the morality of the Scriptures as well as the moral character of the God who inspired them. Several passages are typically given in support of this common feminist objection to the Bible. We've already covered a few of these passages in chapters 2-5. This chapter will explore a few more commonly cited passages and demonstrate how the accusation that the Bible treats women as inferior is without basis.

Coveting Your Neighbor's Wife

The first passage we will look at is the Tenth Commandment:

> You shall not covet your neighbor's house; you shall not covet your neighbor's wife, or his male servant, or his female servant, or his ox, or his donkey, or anything that is your neighbor's. (Exodus 20:17)

This commandment forbids one from yearning for that which belongs to someone else. It includes a list of examples: your neighbor's

---

1   Valerie Tarico, "Owned: Slaves, Women, Children, and Livestock," *Women v. Religion: The Case Against Faith—and for Freedom*. Karen L. Garst, ed. (Durham, NC: Pitchstone Publishing, 2018), p. 100

house, servants, ox, donkey, *and wife*! Based on this verse, feminists argue, according to the perspective of the biblical author, that "a wife is a man's property."[2] After all, she is listed right alongside her husband's animals and material possessions, so it's only logical to assume that the wife is likewise regarded as being "owned" by the husband, right? However, scholars dispute such a reading. According to John Otwell, "The wife here is the first-named member of the household. She is not listed as property, as is so often thought."[3] This interpretation is made all the more clear when we consider the fact that the Bible affirms male-female equality just a few verses earlier in the Fifth Commandment:

> Honor your father and your mother, that your days may be long
> in the land that the Lord your God is giving you. (Exodus 20:12)

Here we see that mother *and* father are equally worthy of honor within the family according to this passage and many others. As Davidson observes, "Far from being regarded as 'chattel,' according to the fifth commandment of the Decalogue and repeated commands throughout the pentateuchal codes, the wife/mother was to be given equal honor to the father within the family circle."[4] Given this fact, it wouldn't make sense for the biblical author to then immediately undermine his own teaching by saying that women are on the same level as houses and animals. Davidson also raises the point that the Torah does not permit a wife to be sold: "[A]n Israelite could sell slaves

---

2   Ibid., p. 111

3   John Otwell, *And Sarah Laughed: The Status of Women in the Old Testament* (Philadelphia, PA: Westminster Press, 1977), p. 76

4   Richard M. Davidson, *Flame of Yahweh: Sexuality in the Old Testament* (Peabody, MA: Hendrickson Publishers, 2007), p. 250

(Exod 21:2-11; Deut 15:12-18) but never his wife, even if she was acquired as a captive in war (Deut 21:14)."[5] Thus, a holistic reading of the Torah reveals that a wife was not considered the property of her husband.

Ritual Impurity

Some feminists might cite the ritual purity legislation, such as laws concerning menstrual impurity (Leviticus 15:19-24), as evidence of sexism in the Bible. It's argued that the Bible regards women as generally unclean and offensive to God because of their physiology.[6] However, they fail to mention that this legislation addresses ritual purity issues that are exclusive to men as well (e.g., Leviticus 15:16). Furthermore, ritual impurity in the Torah does not equate to sinfulness.[7] It's merely a temporary ceremonial status that bars a person from participating in sacred space and activities, such as the tabernacle/temple services in ancient Israel.

---

5 Ibid., p. 249

6 See Lauri Weissman, "Half Human: How Jewish Law Justifies the Exclusion and Exploitation of Women," *Women v. Religion: The Case Against Faith—and for Freedom.* Karen L. Garst, ed. (Durham, NC: Pitchstone Publishing, 2018): "Menstruation, and having a female reproductive system generally, is an impurity and an offense to god, for which women require redemption through regular intervention of male action." (p. 60)

7 See Jonathan Klawans, *Impurity and Sin in Ancient Judaism* (New York, NY: Oxford University Press, 2000): "[T]he following can be said of ritual impurity: It is natural, more or less unavoidable, generally not sinful, and typically impermanent. It is true that the refusal to purify oneself would constitute a transgression, as would coming into contact with the sacred while in a state of ritual impurity. It is also true that a few biblical narratives view "leprosy" as a punishment for moral shortcomings. But in the end, the following claim still stands: It is not sinful to be ritually impure, and ritual impurity does not result from sin" (p. 41)

In regard to the purification period for the birth of a girl being twice as long than for the birth of a boy (Leviticus 12:2-5), consider that the mother brings the same purification offering "whether for a son or for a daughter" (Leviticus 12:6). The Torah intentionally places both son and daughter on the same level; the same offering is required for both of them. Thus, critics overstate their case when they cite this legislation as an example of female inferiority. The reason for the longer purification period for daughters is a matter of "simple mathematical logic." As Davidson explains, "Vaginal bleeding frequently occurs on the part of the newborn girl as well as her mother. Hence, the phrase 'blood purification' likely applies to the discharge of both mother and daughter, and thus the ritual uncleanness of two females must be accounted for."[8]

Ritual impurity was natural and unavoidable for both men and women. When all of the relevant data are considered, the feminist objections on the basis of the ritual purity laws in the Torah are severely underwhelming.

Understanding the Bride-Price

Critics assert that the passages mentioning a "bride-price" entail that the Bible sanctions women being bought and sold as property. In reality, scholars conclude that the bride-price is better translated as "marriage present."[9] It could perhaps be compared, in a small way, to our modern tradition of an engagement ring.

---

8   Richard M. Davidson, *Flame of Yahweh: Sexuality in the Old Testament* (Peabody, MA: Hendrickson Publishers, 2007), p. 246

9   See Daniel I. Block, "Marriage and Family in Ancient Israel," in *Marriage and Family in the Biblical World*, ed. Ken M. Campbell (Downers Grove, IL: InterVarsity, 2003): "When parents deemed their child to be approaching marriageable age, the father of the groom would contact the parents of the potential spouse and negotiate the terms of

The groom-to-be would give this marriage present, which averaged about ten months' wages,[10] to the father of the bride in order to seal the betrothal. Like our modern engagement ring, the bride-price "contributed toward insuring that the marriage was not entered into flippantly."[11] Copan explains that the bride-price "was the way a man showed his serious intentions toward his bride-to-be, and it was a way of bringing two families together to discuss a serious, holy, and lifelong matter."[12]

In the ancient world, the bride-price was a way to express the value of women and the seriousness of marriage and sex, not unlike the preparations and traditions we do today in our modern wedding ceremonies. That is why men who engaged in premarital sexual activity with young women were *still* required to pay the bride-price—even if the young woman's family refused to give her in marriage (Exodus 22:16-17). Having sex without first going through the formal process of marriage disrespected and degraded women, so men who had convinced women to engage in premarital sex were required to make things right.

In addition to bringing the families together, the bride-price served as "compensation to the father for the work the daughter would otherwise have contributed to her family."[13] Furthermore, as Timothy D.

---

the marriage, specifically the nature and size of the mohar, "marriage present." While some have interpreted the mohar as the purchase price, it is preferable to see it as a deposit delivered to the parents of the bride to promote the stability of the marriage and to strengthen the links between the families of those being married." (p. 57)

10   Richard M. Davidson, *Flame of Yahweh: Sexuality in the Old Testament* (Peabody, MA: Hendrickson Publishers, 2007), p. 379

11   Ibid.

12   Paul Copan, *Is God a Moral Monster?: Making Sense of the Old Testament God* (Grand Rapids, MI: Baker Publishing Group, 2011), p. 117

13   Richard M. Davidson, *Flame of Yahweh: Sexuality in the Old Testament* (Peabody, MA:

Terrel observes, the bride-price ultimately didn't belong to the father of the bride but to the bride herself:

> Normally the father of the bride would keep the bride price in trust for his daughter and her children, investing it wisely for their benefit. After his death the fund would go to the daughter for her to manage. Laban's behavior with Rachel and Leah's wealth provides a good example of a breach of that trust (Gen. 31:14-16).[14]

As we have seen, it is a complete misrepresentation of the facts to assert that the Bible sanctions women being bought and sold like property. The bride-price wasn't about "buying" a wife but about demonstrating the serious intentions on the part of the groom-to-be, to express the value of women and marriage, to provide an extra financial investment for the benefit of the young family, and to strengthen family relationships.

Female War Captives

A couple of biblical passages regarding warfare have raised some concerns among modern critics. Feminists, atheists, and others argue that the Bible permits dehumanizing and mistreating women from conquered nations.[15] The two passages on which this objection is based are Numbers 31:15-18 and Deuteronomy 20:13-14.

Hendrickson Publishers, 2007), p. 249

14   Timothy D. Terrell, *Chalcedon*. "Recovering the Bride Price." www.chalcedon.edu. 5/1/2002

15   See Candace Gorham, "Guilt, Shame, and Psychological Pain," *Women v. Religion: The Case Against Faith—and for Freedom*. Karen L. Garst, ed. (Durham, NC: Pitchstone Publishing, 2018): "Essentially, the god of the Old Testament encouraged sex slavery and trafficking." (p. 36)

Regarding the passage from Numbers, critics claim this as an example of the Bible condoning Israelite soldiers enslaving and raping female war captives. (Just as long as the women were virgins!) The passage from Deuteronomy seems to refer to the women from conquered nations as the "spoil" of war that Israelite soldiers can "take as plunder" for themselves, which, according to critics, presumably included permission for the Israelite soldiers to rape them. How do we understand these passages?

We have to keep in mind that these passages weren't written in a vacuum; they need to be understood in light of everything else the Torah says on this topic. Regardless of whether or not they are captives of war, we know that the Torah gives no permission to rape women. Why? First, because the Torah explicitly condemns the act of rape, as we learned in the previous chapter.

Second, the Torah gives specific regulations regarding what to do with a female war captive, which preclude an Israelite solider simply having his way with her. According to Deuteronomy 21:10-14, Israelite soldiers were permitted to *marry* female war captives, but they were forbidden to rape them or treat them as sex objects. Moreover, before they could get married, the woman was to be allowed a month-long period of mourning. According to Daniel Block, "This monthlong quarantine expresses respect for the woman's ties to her family of origin and her own psychological and emotional health, providing a cushion from the shock of being torn from her own family."[16] After this period of mourning, they were permitted to get married and the woman was given full rights as a wife and citizen of Israel. In fact, even in cases where the man changes his mind about marrying her, the Torah

---

16 Daniel Block, *The NIV Application Commentary: Deuteronomy* (Grand Rapids, MI: Zondervan, 2012), p. 496

explicitly prohibits the Israelite soldier from treating the woman as property but rather required that he "let her go where she wants" (Deuteronomy 21:14).

Thus, far from dehumanizing these women, the Torah goes to some length to affirm their dignity and personhood. As John Wenham writes, "In a world where there are wars, and therefore prisoners of war, such regulations in fact set a high standard of conduct."[17]

The Vows of Women

Feminists sometimes complain about the Torah's legislation concerning the husband's/father's right to annul the vows of his wife/daughter in Numbers 30. Feminist author Valerie Tarico cites this legislation as proof that the Bible regards women as lesser beings.[18] However, this legislation doesn't suggest that the Bible considers women to be generally incompetent, as some have alleged. Consider the fact that widows and divorced women were fully permitted to make legally binding vows without the supervision of men (Numbers 30:9). Also, it shouldn't be overlooked that women in ancient Israel "were being given rights that their contemporaries in other societies would largely have not had."[19] The fact that Israelite women were permitted to make legally binding vows at all in this time period is quite significant.

Once again, the purpose of this legislation was ultimately for the protection of vulnerable women. The biblical portrayal of male leader-

---

17   John W. Wenham, *The Goodness of God* (Downers Grove, IL: InterVarsity, 1974), p. 96

18   Valerie Tarico, "Owned: Slaves, Women, Children, and Livestock," *Women v. Religion: The Case Against Faith—and for Freedom*. Karen L. Garst, ed. (Durham, NC: Pitchstone Publishing, 2018), p. 113

19   J.K. McKee, *Men and Women in the Body of Messiah: Answering Crucial Questions* (Richardson, TX: Messianic Apologetics, 2018), p. 224

ship in the family is not one of domination and power over women but of responsibility for those in the husband's/father's loving care. When it came to vows, Davidson explains that the "husband's/father's right to revoke legal commitments of those in his household was a legal prophylactic mechanism to preserve weaker members of society—in particular, the wife or daughter—from consequences that would bring them harm."[20] In an ancient patriarchal culture, women could easily be stepped on and treated unfairly in business transactions, thus the Torah gives fathers and husbands the power to veto such commitments to protect them.

Submission in Marriage

A common feminist complaint is the biblical virtue of submission of wives to husbands (Ephesians 5:22-24). This virtue, feminists argue, demeans and oppresses women.[21] While the Bible certainly extols the virtue of wifely submission, what many feminist critics tend to ignore is that it also extols the virtue of *mutual submission* (Ephesians 5:21), which would involve not only the wife but also the husband having an attitude of submission toward the other. As J.K. McKee explains:

> Submission of a believing wife to a believing husband is to be
> expected (Ephesians 5:22-33; Colossians 3:18-19), but this
> is to be controlled by the overriding statement, "submitting
> to one another out of reverence for Christ" (Ephesians 5:21,
> ESV). Mutual submission also involves the submission of a

---

20 Richard M. Davidson, *Flame of Yahweh: Sexuality in the Old Testament* (Peabody, MA: Hendrickson Publishers, 2007), p. 248

21 Valerie Tarico, "Owned: Slaves, Women, Children, and Livestock," *Women v. Religion: The Case Against Faith—and for Freedom.* Karen L. Garst, ed. (Durham, NC: Pitchstone Publishing, 2018), p. 113

believing husband to his believing wife, and their co-equal, joint leadership of a home together.[22]

Though the instructions for submission are expressed more explicitly for the wife than for the husband, the ideal of mutual submission is not diminished. As Craig Keener points out, "I believe that it is biblically impossible to doubt that Christian husbands and wives should practice mutual submission and servanthood (Eph. 5:21), even if it is specified more explicitly for the wives (v. 22), as all Christians should practice mutual love (v. 2), even if it is specified here more explicitly for the husbands (v. 25)."[23]

Another point that is often ignored by critics is the fact that the husband is charged with loving his wife as Messiah loved the Church, even laying down his life for her (Ephesians 5:25). In the same context that Paul instructs a wife to submit to her husband, he tells a husband to love his wife sacrificially—to love, protect, serve, and provide for her, putting her needs above his own. He is the loving servant-leader of the family, called to emulate the character of Messiah, who came not to be served but to serve (Matthew 20:28). His leadership involves loving his wife as his own body, nourishing and cherishing her (Ephesians 5:28-29).

Finally, as Davidson points out,[24] the Greek term used for "submit" (*hypotassō*), when it occurs in the middle voice, as it does in the

22 J.K. McKee, *Men and Women in the Body of Messiah: Answering Crucial Questions* (Richardson, TX: Messianic Apologetics, 2018), p. 148

23 Craig Keener, "Women in Ministry: Another Egalitarian Perspective," *Two Views on Women in Ministry*. James R. Beck, ed. (Grand Rapids, MI: Zondervan, 2005), p. 242

24 Richard M. Davidson, "Headship, Submission, and Equality in Scripture" in *Women in Ministry: Biblical and Historical Perspectives*. Nancy Vyhmeister, ed. (Berrien Springs, MI: Andrews University Press, 1998), p. 274

context of husband-wife relationships, indicates the wife's voluntary yielding to her husband. Her submission isn't forced by him—in fact, Scripture explicitly commands husbands not to be "harsh" with their wives (Colossians 3:19). These marital imperatives are carried out on the basis of love and respect toward each other (Ephesians 5:33). When we consider the context of this biblical virtue, we see that the reality is a far cry from the feminist characterization of women being treated as inferior beings or as the property of their husbands in the Bible.

But what about 1 Corinthians 11:3, which says that the husband is the "head" of his wife, just as Messiah is the head of the man? The passage even goes on to say that the wife should wear a head covering, lest she bring dishonor to her husband (1 Corinthians 11:5). Most believers today agree that this passage isn't "a transcultural argument in favor of women wearing head coverings in church."[25] Nevertheless, doesn't this passage sanction a general subordination of wives to husbands rather than mutual submission and partnership? Not at all.

First, the passage later goes on to directly affirm male-female equality and interdependence in Messiah: "Nevertheless, in the Lord woman is not independent of man nor man of woman" (1 Corinthians 11:11). Men and women (especially husband and wife) need each other. And just as woman (Eve) came from man (Adam), male children come from women: "for as woman was made from man, so man is now born of woman. And all things are from God" (1 Corinthians 11:12).

Second, the only way to derive the idea of female inferiority or subordination from this passage is to approach the text already assuming it. As Keener contends, "[I]f we want this passage to teach

---

25   Craig Keener, *Paul, Women, & Wives: Marriage and Women's Ministry in the Letters of Paul* (Peabody, MA: Hendrickson Publishers, Inc., 1998), p. 46

subordination, we have to read subordination into the passage."[26] When we read the text without a preconceived bias, this passage is simply saying that a wife should seek to avoid bringing shame upon her family by dressing immodestly. This biblical virtue is not unreasonable—none of us should wish to make our spouse feel uncomfortable by what we wear in public. And it's certainly good to respect dress codes and to try to avoid causing others to stumble. While standards of modesty differ from culture to culture, these principles are still clear and apply to both men and women.

But doesn't the term "head" mean "authority," therefore proving that the Bible commands women "to remain in their proper place behind and beneath men"?[27] While authority is "a possible nuance of the term,"[28] many scholars have suggested that "source" is a more accurate translation of the Greek *kephale*, head, used in 1 Corinthians 11:3.[29] This translation makes sense in light of verse 8, which says that woman was made from man, alluding to the creation narrative in Genesis. Thus, as McKee puts it, "the Messiah is the Creator of the world including the man/Adam, and from the side of the man/Adam came Eve."[30] One objection to this interpretation is that it would entail God is the "source" of Messiah, but this is easily resolved if, as Keener points out, "the text refers to Jesus' source as the Father from

---

26 Ibid., p. 47

27 Valerie Wade, "Black Women and Christianity in the United States: A Historical Perspective, Part 1," *Women v. Religion: The Case Against Faith—and for Freedom*. Karen L. Garst, ed. (Durham, NC: Pitchstone Publishing, 2018), p. 168

28 Craig Keener, *Paul, Women, & Wives: Marriage and Women's Ministry in the Letters of Paul* (Peabody, MA: Hendrickson Publishers, Inc., 1998), p. 34

29 For a more thorough defense of this perspective, see J.K. McKee, *1 Corinthians for the Practical Messianic* (McKinney, TX: Messianic Apologetics, 2015), pp. 233-236

30 J.K. McKee, *Men and Women in the Body of Messiah: Answering Crucial Questions* (Richardson, TX: Messianic Apologetics, 2018), p. 32

whom he proceeded at his incarnation as a human being."[31] Thus, nothing in this passage contradicts the biblical principles of male-female equality and mutual submission.

Women Should Be Seen but Not Heard?

Another complaint you often hear from feminists is that the apostle Paul was a misogynist who prohibited women from speaking in church.[32] This objection is based on a passage from Paul's first letter to the Corinthians:

> The women should keep silent in the churches. For they are not permitted to speak, but should be in submission, as the Law also says. (1 Corinthians 14:34)

A few things must be noted here. First, we cannot claim that this passage represents some kind of general command for women not to speak in church because then Paul would be contradicting himself. Earlier in his letter, Paul mentions women praying and prophesying in church (1 Corinthians 11:5). Since Paul defines prophecy as a spiritual gift intended to edify and instruct the body of believers (1 Corinthians 14:4, 31), this entails that women regularly spoke *and even taught* in church. Moreover, the context of these verses is when "the whole church comes together" (1 Corinthians 14:23). These gatherings involved the church members bringing "a hymn, a lesson, a revela-

---

31 Craig Keener, *Paul, Women, & Wives: Marriage and Women's Ministry in the Letters of Paul* (Peabody, MA: Hendrickson Publishers, Inc., 1998), p. 33

32 Valerie Tarico, "Owned: Slaves, Women, Children, and Livestock," *Women v. Religion: The Case Against Faith—and for Freedom.* Karen L. Garst, ed. (Durham, NC: Pitchstone Publishing, 2018), p. 113

tion, a tongue, or an interpretation" (1 Corinthians 14:26). As Linda Belleville observes:

> Had Paul intended to limit public involvement to men, he surely would have said so here. Instead he emphasizes that women and men alike are to contribute for the upbuilding of the church.[33]

Since women were permitted to prophesy in church, and the context of the verses in question assumes "the whole church" (including women) was involved in bringing "a hymn, a lesson, a revelation, a tongue, or an interpretation" to the gatherings, 1 Corinthians 14:34 cannot be a general command for female silence. The passage must be addressing a specific issue in the Corinthian church, and this is clear in light of the context.

Paul spends the entire chapter instructing the Corinthian church in how to administer orderly worship services (1 Corinthians 14:26, 33, 40). In light of this desire, Paul tells not only women but also men to be silent in certain circumstances (1 Corinthians 14:28, 30). For instance, if someone speaks in tongues, there must be an interpretation, and it must be only one person at a time while everyone else is silent. If there is no one to interpret the tongue, they must "keep silent in church and speak to himself and to God." Prophets must prophesy one by one while the others remain silent. This is because "all things should be done decently and in order" (1 Corinthians 14:40). These calls for both men and women to be silent in particular circumstances obviously does not entail complete silence for the entire service. Therefore,

---

33   Linda Belleville, "Women in Ministry: An Egalitarian Perspective," *Two Views on Women in Ministry.* James R. Beck, ed. (Grand Rapids, MI: Zondervan, 2005), p. 71

neither should we interpret 1 Corinthians 14:34 as a general command for total female silence in church.

Furthermore, Paul isn't addressing women in general but only certain Corinthian wives. This is made clear in verse 35 when he references their husbands. These particular wives whom Paul is addressing must have been engaging in some sort of speech that was disruptive to the service. Perhaps there was an issue of wives interrupting as their husbands' prophecies were being weighed by the other prophets. Whatever the situation may have been, Paul's solution is that these particular Corinthian wives were to ask their questions at home rather than disrupt the orderly flow of the service (1 Corinthians 14:35).

Again, Paul's intention was to prevent both men and women from bringing disorder to the service, so he gave practical guidance to help the Corinthian church administer orderly worship services. As we've seen in other parts of Paul's letter to the Corinthians—and even in chapter 14 itself—women were permitted to speak in church. Therefore, 1 Corinthians 14:34 cannot be a general command for female silence during worship services.

When we look at the evidence honestly, nothing in Scripture suggests that women are inferior to men or considered male property. Even the difficult passages affirm the value of women in God's eyes.

CHAPTER 7
DOES THE BIBLE EXCLUDE WOMEN FROM MINISTRY?

Can women preach God's word and serve in congregational leadership, or are these duties and positions restricted to only men? Many feminist critics of Christianity are under the impression that Scripture bans women from participating in any sort of ministry leadership, and this is often cited as an example of male-female inequality and even sexism.[1] But does the Bible really prohibit qualified women from preaching and leading within the congregation or via public ministry?[2]

---

1   See Alexis Record, "Women v. Indoctrination," *Women v. Religion: The Case Against Faith—and for Freedom*. Karen L. Garst, ed. (Durham, NC: Pitchstone Publishing, 2018): "It doesn't take a bunch of studies to see sexism in religion. All we have to do is look at the dearth of women in positions of authority within major religious institutions to get an idea of how they are viewed […] Compared to hostile sexism, which will insult or antagonize women outright, benevolent sexism will compliment them in a childlike or prejudiced way based on stereotypes. The Bible does this when it labels the wife the "weaker vessel" compared to the husband (1 Peter 3:7). Even when "weaker" was interpreted in my church as 'more precious and valuable' it still meant women weren't equal to men and were kept away from responsibilities and leadership." (p. 87-88)

2   It should be noted that Christianity is divided regarding the extent to which women can hold leadership positions within the Church. The view that some offices within the Church (e.g., elder/pastor) are restricted to men is known as complementarianism. However, even complementarian theology affirms the ontological equality of men and women in addition to broadly permitting women to serve in various leadership roles within the areas of teaching, evangelism, etc. The view that Scripture does not prohibit qualified women from high leadership positions within the Church is called egalitarianism, which is the view I hold. For a more thorough defense of egalitarianism and critique of complementarianism, see J.K. McKee, *Men and Women in the Body of Messiah: Answering Crucial Questions* (Richardson, TX: Messianic Apologetics, 2018)

The question of women's involvement in ministry concerns not only critics but also Christians. If God has called some women to certain areas of ministry leadership, but men restrict women from serving in those areas to which they are called, it does a disservice to the work of the Church. Before we unpack the one passage that appears to ban women from public teaching and leadership (1 Timothy 2:12), it's worthwhile to consider the plethora of biblical examples that demonstrate the contrary. Since I don't believe the Bible contradicts itself regarding this issue, my approach will be to explore how this one difficult passage can be reconciled in light of the many clear passages.

Biblical Evidence Supporting Women in Ministry

If we read the Bible from start to finish, without any preconceived bias, it's hard to conclude that female ministers are somehow "unbiblical." To draw that conclusion, you would have to ignore the Bible's many direct references to female prophets, teachers, apostles, judges, worship leaders, etc. The Bible plainly states that women held leadership roles in both Old and New Testaments, including leadership over men, and none of these references offer any note of condemnation.

Consider Miriam, the sister of Moses and Aaron. The Bible identifies her as a leader and prophetess of Israel alongside her brothers. She was directly "sent" by the Lord Himself to lead Israel in the wilderness (Micah 6:4). If Miriam's public leadership were against God's will, we would expect some sort of explicit or implicit rebuke in Scripture. Instead, the Scriptures matter-of-factly present her as a

---

and Craig Keener, *Paul, Women, & Wives: Marriage and Women's Ministry in the Letters of Paul* (Peabody, MA: Hendrickson Publishers, Inc., 1998)

leader without any indication that her position violated God's will. Miriam's leadership role referenced in Micah 6:4 is particularly important because, as Belleville observes, "it shows that Miriam's role was traditionally and historically understood as a leadership one by the community of faith centuries later."[3]

Consider Deborah, who is recognized as a prominent judge in Israel, "thus holding the highest position of authority in her time."[4] She exercised authority over both men and women who came to her to have their disputes resolved (Judges 4:4-5). She also served in the role of prophetess, which entails spiritual authority in addition to governmental authority. She is labeled a "mother in Israel" (Judges 5:7), which might be an honorific title for an authority figure or protector in the community.[5] Again, the biblical text presents Deborah as a leader of God's people without any indication that this was improper.

Consider Huldah, who was a prophetess and the head advisor to King Josiah (2 Kings 22:14-20; 2 Chronicles 34:22-28). Her prophecy authenticated the authority of the written Torah that was found in the house of the Lord (2 Chronicles 34:14, 24), which is quite a significant moment in both Jewish and Christian theology. Scholar Claudia V. Camp remarks:

---

3   Linda Belleville, "Women in Ministry: An Egalitarian Perspective," *Two Views on Women in Ministry*. James R. Beck, ed. (Zondervan, 2005), p. 51

4   Craig Keener, *Paul, Women, & Wives: Marriage and Women's Ministry in the Letters of Paul* (Peabody, MA: Hendrickson Publishers, Inc., 1998) p. 244

5   Tikva Fymer-Kensky, "Deborah," *Women in Scripture: A Dictionary of Names and Unnamed Women in the Hebrew Bible, the Apocryphal/Deuterocanonical Books, and the New Testament*. Carol Meryers, ed. (Grand Rapids, MI: Eerdmans, 2000)

> Huldah's story is notable in the biblical tradition in that her prophetic words of judgment are centered on a written document: she authorizes what will become the core of Scripture for Judaism and Christianity. Her validation of a text thus stands as the first recognizable act in the long process of canon formation. Huldah authenticates a document as being God's word, thereby affording it the sanctity required for establishing a text as authoritative, or canonical.[6]

These examples alone demonstrate that the Old Testament didn't prohibit qualified women from serving in high-level leadership roles. Some opponents of women's ministry might object and say that these women are mere "exceptions" and not to be counted as normative. However, as Keener argues, once one concedes that exceptions to their rule exist, "they have forfeited their right to pass judgment on any particular woman's call."[7] In any case, the Old Testament doesn't exclude women from ministry.

The New Testament likewise has no shortage of female leaders and teachers. The book of Acts declares that God poured out His Spirit on His people and that both "sons and daughters" were empowered to prophesy (Acts 2:17-18; Joel 2:28-29). Paul fully affirmed women's public prayer and prophesying in the church (1 Corinthians 11:4-5), and the New Testament mentions several female prophets, such as Anna and Philip's four daughters (Luke 2:36; Acts 21:9). Some critics might object that while women were permitted to prophesy, they still weren't allowed to teach the Scriptures or function in a pastoral

---

6   Claudia V. Camp, "Huldah," Ibid.

7   Craig Keener, *Paul, Women, & Wives: Marriage and Women's Ministry in the Letters of Paul* (Peabody, MA: Hendrickson Publishers, Inc., 1998) pp. 248-249

role. However, prophecy, by definition, is delivering a message from God to the people "so that all may learn and all be encouraged" (1 Corinthians 14:31). Thus, prophecy includes instructing (teaching) believers regarding God's will, and there is no reason to think this wouldn't include appeal to the Scriptures—the prophets in the Old Testament appealed to the Torah all the time. Additionally, as Keener points out, prophets and teachers "were more prominent than local pastors" and, in some churches, "apparently were the pastors (Acts 13:1)."[8] If someone thought that the Bible bans female ministers, these facts should at least give them pause.

In addition to prophetesses, the New Testament also notes other female ministers, such as the missionary Priscilla, whom Paul calls his "fellow worker" in ministry (Romans 16:3). Paul commends her and her husband, Aquila, for risking their lives for him (Romans 16:4). Priscilla is also described as a facilitator of a home church (1 Corinthians 16:9) and a teacher (Acts 18:26).

In addition to missionaries and teachers, the New Testament also notes another female in a high-level position of leadership: Junia, who is "outstanding among the apostles" (Romans 16:7, NASB). Some have suggested that Junia is not actually a feminine name, but the support for this view is extremely weak.[9] Others have suggested that

---

8   Craig Keener, "Women in Ministry: Another Egalitarian Perspective," *Two Views on Women in Ministry.* James R. Beck, ed. (Grand Rapids, MI: Zondervan, 2005), p. 214

9   See Craig Keener, *Paul, Women, & Wives: Marriage and Women's Ministry in the Letters of Paul* (Peabody, MA: Hendrickson Publishers, Inc., 1998): "Since the text suggests that Junia was an apostles, some have debated whether 'Junia' is really a feminine name; the RSV simply assumes that it is not by translating 'men of note among the apostles'— even though there is little to support this translation but the opinion of the translators that a woman could not be an apostles. Although the name as it occurs here could be a contraction for the masculine Junianus, there is no evidence for this in extant Roman inscriptions, and the most natural way to read the name is 'Junia,' a common enough

the verse should say that Junia was merely "well known to the apostles" (Romans 16:7, ESV), but again, the textual evidence simply doesn't bear this out.[10] Paul's praise of Junia as an apostle would entail that women were permitted to serve in such high-level ministry positions. Apostles essentially functioned as church planters[11] who provided ongoing pastoral guidance to local congregations and "exercised more authority (charismatic, but continuous) than local elders."[12]

In addition to apostles, the New Testament also acknowledges women serving as evangelists. Euodia and Synthyche are called fellow laborers in the Gospel, serving alongside Paul himself (Philippians 4:2-3). According to Belleville, "these women were not only co-evangelists but key leaders of the Philippian church."[13] Paul's instruction to the "true companion" in verse 3 to help these women

---

woman's name." (pp. 241-242)

10   See ibid: "It is also unnatural to read the text as merely claiming that they had a high reputation with 'the apostles.' Since they were imprisoned with him, Paul knows them well enough to recommend them without appealing to the other apostles, whose judgment he never cites on such matters, and the Greek is most naturally read as claiming that they were apostles." (p. 242)

11   See Linda Belleville, *Women Leaders and the Church: Three Crucial Questions* (Grand Rapids, MI: Baker Books, 2000): "Paul's broader usage leads us to think that apostle was similar in function to a church planter. For one, the term appears in contexts that stress the person's role as a coworker in the church planting process (e.g., 1 Cor. 9:1-6; 1 Thess. 2:6-8). As 'apostles of Christ,' Paul, Silas, and Timothy could have been a financial burden on the newly founded Thessalonian church but waived this right (1 Thess. 1:1; 2:6-7). It also fits with Paul's understanding of the church as a house that is 'built on the foundation of the apostles and prophets' (Eph. 2:20)." (p. 54)

12   Craig Keener, "A Response to Craig Blomberg," *Two Views on Women in Ministry*. James R. Beck, ed. (Grand Rapids, MI: Zondervan, 2005), p. 186

13   Linda Belleville, *Women Leaders and the Church: Three Crucial Questions* (Grand Rapids, MI: Baker Books, 2000), p. 60

work out their differences indicates that "their role was so important that their disagreement put the unity of the church in jeopardy."[14]

So far, we've seen that women in the New Testament served as prophetesses, teachers, missionaries, apostles, and evangelists. But wait! There's more! Phoebe, the courier of Paul's epistle to the community of believers in Rome, is identified as a "deacon" (Romans 16:1). Since she was the bearer of Paul's letter to the Romans, "she may be called upon to explain anything ambiguous in the letter when the Romans read it, and Paul wishes them to understand that she is indeed qualified to explain his writing."[15] To reassure his readers that Phoebe was equipped to explain his teaching, Paul cites her credentials as a leader within the church at Cenchreae. Being a deacon required that one be, among other things, committed to sound doctrine (1 Timothy 3:9).

In conclusion, we have seen ample Old and New Testament evidence that nothing banned women from teaching nor holding high leadership positions within the believing community. Women served in many of the same ministry roles as men without the slightest hint of divine disapproval.

Biblical Evidence Allegedly Opposed to Women in Ministry

Before we get to the one biblical passage that appears to ban women from public teaching and leadership, let's address the one religious office from which women were certainly excluded: the Levitical priesthood. Some argue by analogy that, since women weren't permitted to serve in the priesthood, they are likewise prohibited from other ministry roles,

---

14   Ibid.

15   Craig Keener, *Paul, Women, & Wives: Marriage and Women's Ministry in the Letters of Paul* (Peabody, MA: Hendrickson Publishers, Inc., 1998) pp. 248-238

such as pastor and teacher. However, this analogy breaks down in a couple of ways.

First, not only women but also most men were excluded from serving in the Levitical priesthood. For example, men who weren't from the tribe of Levi and the line of Aaron couldn't serve in the priesthood. Neither could men who were "blind or lame," or men who had a "mutilated face or limb too long," or men who were a "hunchback or a dwarf" (Leviticus 21:18-20). And yet, nobody would say that any of these conditions disqualify men from ministering as pastors or teachers today.

Second, the New Testament applies the priesthood analogy to *all* believers, both male and female. Peter taught that believers "are being built up as a spiritual house, to be a holy priesthood" (1 Peter 2:5). In direct reference to Exodus 19:6, Peter calls believers in Messiah "a royal priesthood, a holy nation" (1 Peter 2:9). Believers who take part in the first resurrection "will be priests of God and of Christ" during the millennial reign of Messiah (Revelation 20:6). Since the Bible applies the analogy to all believers, it doesn't make sense to appeal to the Levitical priesthood as an argument to limit women's ministry roles.

So why were women restricted from serving in the Levitical priesthood? There is a logical reason for this: the Torah's purity legislation made female participation in the priesthood impractical.[16] The ritual purity legislation governing menstruation and childbirth barred women from the tabernacle/temple often and for long periods of time. It should be noted, however, that among the duties that priests

---

16   See Craig Keener, "Women in Ministry: Another Egalitarian Perspective," *Two Views on Women in Ministry*. James R. Beck, ed. (Grand Rapids, MI: Zondervan, 2005): "The law's stricter purity restrictions for women (esp. regarding menstruation) made women priests impractical (in a system which would disqualify them from service for considerable periods of time)." (p. 186)

fulfilled, women (along with most men) in ancient Israel would have been prohibited only from fulfilling certain cultic rituals in the tabernacle/temple. That's it. Other duties often performed by priests, such as teaching, adjudication, and prophecy were not restricted to men alone, as we've seen with women like Deborah and Huldah. Therefore, the Levitical priesthood gives us no basis for prohibiting women from teaching or pastoral ministry.

A similar argument by analogy is sometimes made in regard to Yeshua's disciples. Since Yeshua's twelve disciples were all male, the Bible thereby excludes women from ministry. However, once again, this analogy breaks down. If we are going to exclude women from ministry based on the characteristics of the twelve disciples, then by that same logic we must also exclude non-Jewish men since the disciples were all Jewish. Obviously, nobody believes that the Bible prohibits non-Jews from teaching and leadership; it's just as absurd to exclude women on the basis that the disciples were all male.

However, one relevant passage in the New Testament can easily be taken to mean that women are banned from teaching and holding positions of authority over men in the church. That passage is found in Paul's first letter to Timothy:

> Let a woman learn quietly with all submissiveness. I do not permit a woman to teach or to exercise authority over a man; rather, she is to remain quiet. For Adam was formed first, then Eve; and Adam was not deceived, but the woman was deceived and became a transgressor. Yet she will be saved through childbearing—if they continue in faith and love and holiness, with self-control. (1 Timothy 2:11-15)

This is certainly a difficult passage that requires careful examination. To begin, let's establish the context. Paul is writing to Timothy who was in Ephesus (1:3). Much of the purpose of Paul's letter was to direct Timothy in countering errant teachings that were negatively affecting the believing community in Ephesus (1:3-7; 4:1-4; 6:3-5). Paul's instructions were that Timothy should teach and bring correction to the community (4:6-16) and establish solid leaders to help care for the church and address error (3:1-13).

Paul's admonitions in the second chapter of his letter must be understood against this backdrop. Ultimately, Paul's goal is to instruct Timothy on how to confront those who are stirring up division and strife within the community through their false teachings and bad behavior.

With that in mind, Paul begins chapter 2 by urging public prayer for kings and those in positions of authority (2:1-2). This is to encourage peaceful and quiet living among the believers so that their witness to the truth of the Gospel wouldn't be hindered (2:3-7). Paul then specifically addresses the men in the community, exhorting them to pray "without anger or quarreling" (2:8), indicating that perhaps there was a general problem with anger and conflict among the men in Ephesus (see 6:4-5). Paul then turns to address issues related specifically to the women in the community. The first issue is in regard to their dress (2:9-10), suggesting that perhaps there was a general problem of inappropriate dress among the women in Ephesus. Keener explains that Paul's concern was with people "adorning themselves to attract glances from congregants of the opposite gender or to show off their wealth or new fashions in church,"[17] which

---

17   Craig Keener, *Paul, Women, & Wives: Marriage and Women's Ministry in the Letters of Paul* (Peabody, MA: Hendrickson Publishers, Inc., 1998), p. 103

apparently caused such disruption within the community to warrant this correction.

Now we get to the main passage in question, which is Paul's second corrective instruction regarding the women at Ephesus. Let's unpack this passage verse-by-verse.

Let a woman learn quietly with all submissiveness. (1 Timothy 2:11)

The first thing worth highlighting here is that Paul fully expects women to learn! "Let a woman learn" is an imperative to teach women, which was pretty radical in a culture that widely deemphasized women's education. Tim Hegg explains that the majority of the Sages at this time "generally felt that Torah study should be left primarily for the men."[18] Paul followed in the footsteps of His Messiah and Lord, Yeshua, who likewise defied cultural expectations by affirming the education of women (Luke 10:39-41), taking the minority view which "stressed equality among men and women in matters of study and training"[19] within an otherwise unobliging religious atmosphere.

Second, what does Paul mean when he says that the women should learn "quietly"? The Greek term *hesuchia*, translated "quietly," has a range of meaning "from absolute silence to quietness (or peacefulness) of spirit to silence (or quietness) in respect of some speaking activity (here teaching, but elsewhere of being silent while another speaks, Acts 22:2)."[20] In this context, the word simply means "quiet, calm, not disruptive." This is followed by "with all submissiveness." Submissiveness

---

18 Tim Hegg, *The Role of Women in the Messianic Assembly* (Tacoma, WA: TorahResource, 1988), p. 37

19 Ibid.

20 Philip H. Towner, *The New International Commentary on the New Testament: The Letters to Timothy and Titus* (Grand Rapids, MI: Wm. B. Eerdmans Publishing Co., 2006), p. 214

in regard to whom? In this learning context, it makes the most sense to think of this imperative as applying to teachers/leaders. In other words, in a learning environment, the women in view must be quiet, attentive, and not disruptive; they must submit to the leaders in the community and humbly accept their teaching. It's easy to see how this attitude of quietness and submissiveness is appropriate for both men and women in such a learning environment. Paul earlier exhorts *everyone* in the church to lead peaceful and quiet lives (2:2).

> I do not permit a woman to teach or to exercise authority over
> a man; rather, she is to remain quiet. (2 Timothy 2:12)

This verse, according to Keener, is "the only explicit prohibition in the entire Bible against women teaching."[21] Thus, it's no wonder that it is at the center of the debate regarding women teaching and holding positions of leadership. But is this verse a universal ban on female ministers? If that is the case, then we have some problems. As we've already covered, Paul himself commended female leaders and teachers (Romans 16:1, 3, 7; Philippians 4:2-3). So something more must be going on here.

Instead of viewing the plethora of examples of female ministers in the Bible as exceptions to the rule against women's ministry, we should instead view 1 Timothy 2:12 as the exception to the rule affirming women's ministry. That is to say, according to a holistic reading of the Bible, women are generally allowed to serve in teaching and leadership roles but restricted in certain exceptional situations. 1 Timothy 2:12 represents not the rule but an *exceptional case* in which women were

---

21 Craig Keener, *Paul, Women, & Wives: Marriage and Women's Ministry in the Letters of Paul* (Peabody, MA: Hendrickson Publishers, Inc., 1998), p. 101

prohibited from teaching and serving in leadership positions within the church.

But why did Paul issue a ban in this specific case? The reason, as Paul explains, is that there were ignorant people in Ephesus teaching falsely (1:4-7)—and, apparently, these false teachers often targeted vulnerable women, such as young widows (2 Timothy 3:6), who would then spread their false teachings (5:13). Thus, Paul's solution for this specific problem was twofold: first, the Ephesian women must be barred from teaching and assuming authority in the congregation. Second, they must learn quietly from reliable teachers and leaders (2:11).[22] If we are to glean any general principle from this passage to be applied today, it is not that women should be excluded from ministry. The principle for today is that unqualified women *and men* who are known to believe and spread false teachings are not to be given a position of influence within the church.

While I think this approach makes the most sense of all the data, we aren't out of the woods yet! Paul now moves on to substantiate his teaching in light of the Torah:

> For Adam was formed first, then Eve; and Adam was not deceived, but the woman was deceived and became a transgressor. Yet she will be saved through childbearing—if they continue in faith and love and holiness, with self-control. (2 Timothy 2:13-15)

---

22   See Ibid: "Presumably, Paul wants them to learn so that they could *teach*. If he prohibits women from teaching because they are unlearned, his demand that they learn constitutes a long-range solution to the problem. Women unlearned in the Bible could not be trusted to pass on its teachings accurately, but once they had learned, this would not be an issue, and they could join the ranks of women colleagues in ministry whom Paul elsewhere commends." (p. 112)

Some take these verses to mean that women are prohibited from teaching and leadership because, based on the example we have with Eve, they are deceived more easily than men. But is that really what Paul is saying? Did Paul consider all women, by virtue of their femaleness, to be easily deceived and thus not mentally equipped for teaching/leadership? If he did, we have some inconsistencies. For instance, why does Paul commend the ministry of several female ministers? And why does he explicitly instruct the older women to teach the younger women? (Titus 2:3-4) If women in general were easily deceived, it would stand to reason that Paul wouldn't want women teaching anyone!

Again, these verses must be understood to be primarily about the local situation in Ephesus. Paul applied the illustration of Eve being deceived not to women in general but only to the unlearned Ephesian women addressed in his letter. Just as Eve was targeted by the serpent, the Ephesian women were being targeted by false teachers. Also, we know that Paul didn't consider Eve to be a symbol for all women because he applies this same analogy of Eve being deceived to both men and women at the church of Corinth (2 Corinthians 11:3). Eve did not represent all women in all times but rather served as a symbol for easily deceived believers, whether they be male or female. The principle for today, therefore, is not that women are easily deceived and thus shouldn't teach/lead; it's that we must not permit unlearned and easily deceived women *or men* to hold positions of influence in the church.

What does Paul mean when he says that "she will be saved through childbearing"? Feminist critics have accused the Bible of teaching that women atone for their sins by having and raising children.[23] Obviously this verse cannot be teaching salvation by motherhood—that would contradict everything else Paul teaches about salvation being by grace through faith in Messiah alone, not by works. So what's going on here?

J.K. McKee offers a reasonable solution by pointing out the definite article present in the Greek clause commonly rendered "through childbearing."[24] According to McKee, a literal translation would be "through the child-bearing." Based on this and other textual factors, McKee concludes, "There is strong support for the salvation referred to not coming via the process of raising children, but rather with this being a statement about the Incarnation and birth of Yeshua the Messiah."[25] This explanation makes perfect sense in light of Paul's reference to Adam and Eve and the fall in Genesis 3. Right after sin entered the world through Adam and Eve, the first promise of salvation was proclaimed, and it would come forth through the seed of the woman (Genesis 3:15). This promised seed has arrived via the Incarnation and birth of the Messiah. Thus, Paul's hope for these Ephesian women who were being deceived and spreading false teaching was

---

23   Valerie Tarico, "Owned: Slaves, Women, Children, and Livestock," *Women v. Religion: The Case Against Faith—and for Freedom.* Karen L. Garst, ed. (Durham, NC: Pitchstone Publishing, 2018), p. 113

24   See J.K. McKee, *Men and Women in the Body of Messiah: Answering Crucial Questions* (Richardson, TX: Messianic Apologetics, 2018): "The Apostle Paul does not say that women are to be saved through having children, and neither does he say that motherhood is somehow akin to women working out their salvation. This is quite apparent when one looks at the Greek clause commonly rendered as "through childbearing" (CJB), *dia tēs teknogonias.* Of notable significance to us is the presence of the definite article *tēs,* attached to the noun *teknogonias.* A literal translation of *dia tēs teknogonias* can legitimately be "through the child-bearing." (p. 244)

25   Ibid.

that they would learn from qualified teachers. Then, by coming to a knowledge of the promised Savior, they may repent and be saved.

In conclusion, no, the Bible does not exclude qualified women from ministry. We've seen several examples in Scripture of qualified women serving in many of the same ministry roles as men. Additionally, we've seen that the one passage that is often taken to mean that women's ministry roles are restricted is actually *not* a general restriction on women's ministry at all. Contrary to the claims of some, the Bible fully allows for qualified women teaching and serving in high leadership positions within the church.

CHAPTER 8
CHRISTIANITY VS. FEMINISM: WHICH IS BETTER FOR WOMEN?

In this book, we've countered many feminist objections against Christianity and the Bible. We've seen that the Bible fully affirms male-female equality, justice, and protection for women. Never does the Bible teach that women are inferior to men or are male property. Still, many secular feminists will insist that one must abandon their Christian beliefs and convictions if they genuinely believe in women's rights.[1] Christianity, at best, hinders women's progress, and at worst, directly opposes it. Feminism, on the other hand, liberates and elevates women—or so it is said. But is that true?

First, it's worth mentioning that many Christians throughout history have held unbiblical views on women, and this is still true of some fundamentalist segments of Christianity today. Not all feminists are angry for no reason. Many are coming from a place of painful experience. They were exposed to a distorted version of Christianity that has misrepresented the Bible when it comes to how women should be treated. For these women, their problem isn't with the Bible but with what they've been led to believe the Bible says. Religious leaders have falsely taught, either overtly or subtly, that women are inferior

---

1   See Lauri Weissman, "Half Human: How Jewish Law Justifies the Exclusion and Exploitation of Women," *Women v. Religion: The Case Against Faith—and for Freedom*. Karen L. Garst, ed. (Durham, NC: Pitchstone Publishing, 2018): "Vocal feminism and atheism now are moral obligations: anything less makes us complicit in the dehumanization, commoditization, and sexual exploitation of women. To protect the defenseless and progress toward humanism, women must abandon religion." (p. 72)

in the eyes of God—and then critics of Christianity later regurgitated these false teachings.

The truth is that the Bible, like women, has often suffered from the abuse of men. In many ways, the Bible has been misinterpreted and used to oppress women. When modern feminists complain about Christianity, much of the time, they are reacting to the distorted, unbiblical version of it. But I don't care to defend unbiblical religions. The question is between *biblical* Christianity and modern feminism: which is better for women?

Is Secular Feminism the Answer to Female Oppression?

Women doubtless still face oppression, even in our progressive western culture. We need to look no further than Harvey Weinstein, the famous film producer who was exposed as a serial sexual abuser just a couple of years ago. The allegations against him sparked what has come to be called the #MeToo Movement, which has since been shining a bright light on how countless women are mistreated and abused by powerful men. Since this movement erupted in our culture, it seems like every other week a new scumbag is exposed for his sexual harassment and abuse against women—a parade of scumbags. Of course, we also can't forget to mention men like Jeffrey Epstein and Larry Nassar, who have likewise abused hundreds of women, as it has been recently uncovered. And these are just the most famous cases.

In light of these recent events, a couple of observations can be made. First, despite all of our social progress in the West, women are still being abused and degraded by men. This is taking place even in places like Hollywood, the media, and at the highest levels of political office—places that fully promote feminist values and are supposedly run by the most enlightened among us. Indeed, even in these "progressive" environments, women are still treated as objects. Dr. Katie McCoy summarizes this point well:

> We women can vote, own businesses, pursue any education-
> al or vocational field, be CEOs of fortune 500 companies,
> university presidents, and US senators. But we still have to
> be careful going to the grocery store at night. We still have to
> walk fast with our eyes forward and pray that the catcalling
> men don't become aggressive. We still have to be hyper-vigilant
> in a parking garage. For all of the social activism of the last
> sixty years, rape culture, sexual harassment, and misogyny have
> not been educated out of society or reformed away. For all of
> our social progress, humanity's core still remains unchanged,
> and for all of our social advantages, women still face oppres-
> sion and sexual abuse. That women have achieved unparalleled
> independence, yet still contend for basic safety and public
> value, is a sobering cultural commentary.[2]

What does this tell us? Frankly, despite all of our social progress, the secular feminist movement has been utterly ineffective in solving the issue of female oppression. Women are still mistreated and degrad-ed in our culture. Why? How is it that we've come so far in our society, and yet women are still being mistreated? The reason for this is quite simple: female oppression is a *moral* issue. Again, as McCoy rightly notes, "humanity's core still remains unchanged."

This leads to a second observation: our society is crying out for justice. We all recognize that it's morally wrong to abuse and degrade

---

2   Katie McCoy, *SWBTS Libraries*. "Elliott Coffee Talk." https://youtu.be/bu8PBIxiuUA. Accessed 10/10/2019

women, hence the #MeToo Movement. We all recognize that we have a moral duty to protect the vulnerable. But these convictions assume an objective moral standard. The problem is that secular feminism gives us no basis for these moral values and obligations. If there is no God, then there is no standard.

Indeed, if atheism is true, then on what basis do women or men have any objective moral worth at all? We're merely "the accidental by-product of nature, a result of matter plus time plus chance."[3] We've all evolved from primordial goo for no reason or purpose, just the same as mosquitoes and rats. Therefore, why should we treat human beings as special? Where do we get these delusions that we have these moral obligations toward one another—that people have intrinsic dignity and are worthy of respect? After all, on the atheistic view, humans are just animals, "machines created by our genes."[4] And animals have no moral duties or prohibitions.

Think about it: we don't condemn male dolphins as abusive gang rapists when they isolate a female dolphin, slap her around with their tails, and forcibly copulate with her for weeks. Why not? Because they are just being animals. If humans are just highly evolved animals, why do we think the standards should be different for human behavior? If life is just an accident of nature, and there is no God who has a purpose for our lives, we can't say that rape and sexual assault are wrong in any meaningful way. Without God, we have no basis to condemn the behavior of people like Harvey Weinstein, Jeffrey Epstein, and all the rest. As atheist Richard Dawkins writes, "Much as we might wish

---

3   William Lane Craig, *Reasonable Faith: Christian Truth and Apologetics* (Wheaton, IL: Crossway Books, 2008) p. 71

4   Richard Dawkins, *The Selfish Gene* (Oxford University Press, 1989), p. 2

to believe otherwise, universal love and the welfare of species as a whole are concepts which simply do not make evolutionary sense."[5]

It gets worse. According to a paper published by the New York Academy of Sciences titled "Why Men Rape," two evolutionary sociobiologists named Randy Thornhill and Craig Palmer wrote that rape is actually "a natural, biological phenomenon that is a product of the human evolutionary heritage."[6] Rape evolved as a "reproductive strategy"—a man who couldn't get a woman to agree to mate with him would simply force her to.

Therefore, if life came about only through natural selection, and if our human behavior is shaped according to what is needed to survive and pass on our genes—in this case, the strong sexually overpowering the weak—then sexual assault not only has no basis for being morally wrong but is also necessary for human survival! Again, atheistic naturalism gives us no real basis for the conviction that women have moral worth and should be protected.

Now, even though atheism and secular feminism can't explain *why* acts like rape are wrong, everyone agrees that they *are* wrong. In their paper, Thornhill and Palmer are quick to declare that while they believe rape is natural and biological, they don't mean to suggest that such behavior is justified. So what is their solution to the problem of rape? What they propose is "an evolutionarily informed program for young men that teaches them to restrain their sexual behavior."[7] They envision a young man taking this course before he gets his driver's license. The course will inform him of his evolved sexual proclivity

---

5   Ibid.

6   Randy Thornhill, Craig T. Palmer, "Why Men Rape," *The New York Academy of Sciences*, Vol. 40, No. 1 (2000), pp. 30-36

7   Ibid.

toward rape. "Most of all," Thornhill and Palmer say, "the program should stress that a man's evolved sexual desires offer him no excuse whatsoever for raping a woman, and that if he understands and resists those desires, he may be able to prevent their manifestation in sexually coercive behavior."[8]

In other words, if men understand how their brains have evolved, they *might* be able to stop themselves from raping. Again, human beings are merely animals. And if men understand that they are animals, maybe they'll learn to behave *not* like animals. We're all purposeless bags of meat who rape to survive—maybe we should restrain our natural impulses and be nice to each other *just because*. That's the "solution" that naturalism gives us. In either case, the underlying assumption of Thornhill and Palmer's suggestion is that rape is wrong, which again, cannot be explained on a naturalistic worldview. As Dr. McCoy eloquently puts it:

> Even this suggestion [from Thornhill and Palmer] implies a moral code that is incongruent with purely biological explanations for such sexually coercive behavior. If sexual assault is an adaptation, upon what moral basis would a man attempt to "prevent its manifestation"? Upon what moral basis would a government even penalize a man for such a crime? After all, maybe his brain made him do it.[9]

---

8   Ibid.
9   Katie McCoy, *SWBTS Libraries*. "Elliott Coffee Talk." https://youtu.be/bu8PBIxiuUA. Accessed 10/10/2019

Without God, the belief that life originated and evolved via purely natural causes is "the only game in town."[10] And as we've seen, there is simply no objective basis for female dignity and moral behavior within such a naturalistic worldview. Slogans that men should "do better" are thus meaningless. Secular feminism cannot bring about true change in the human heart whereby women are valued and protected in society.

Secular feminism not only fails to provide any basis for the moral worth of women but also maintains ideals that devalue and harm women. Take, for instance, modern feminism's highest sacrament: abortion. Countless female babies are being slaughtered in the womb every day while today's feminists cheer. The most obvious problem with this feminist ideal is that nothing says you hate women more than advocating for the "right" to murder them. But this is exactly what modern feminists fiercely endorse and fight for. "Shout your abortion!"[11] feminists proclaim. "Free abortions on demand and without apology!"[12] they chant at their protests. One feminist author, Mary Elizabeth Williams, candidly admits that a fetus is a human life. And yet, her affirmation of that fact "doesn't make [her] one iota less solidly pro-choice."[13] She goes on to say this:

> Here's the complicated reality in which we live: All life is not
> equal. That's a difficult thing for liberals like me to talk about,

---

10 Alvin Plantinga, "When Faith and Reason Clash: Evolution and the Bible," *Christian Scholar's Review*, XXI:1 (1991), pp. 8-33

11 Tamar Lewin, *The New York Times*. "#ShoutYourAbortion Gets Angry Shouts Back." www.nytimes.com. Accessed 12/12/19

12 Jessica Valenti, *The Nation*. "Free Abortion on Demand Without Apology." www.thenation.com. Accessed 12/12/19

13 Mary Elizabeth Williams, *Salon*. "So what is abortion ends life?" www.salon.com. Accessed 12/12/19

lest we wind up looking like death-panel-loving, kill-your-grandma-and-your-precious-baby storm troopers. Yet a fetus can be a human life without having the same rights as the woman in whose body it resides. She's the boss. Her life and what is right for her circumstances and her health should automatically trump the rights of the non-autonomous entity inside of her. Always.[14]

According to modern feminism, *some* girls don't deserve equal rights. Modern feminists cannot therefore claim to fight for the rights of women since they actively fight *against* the rights of *some* women—namely, the rights of baby girls inside of the womb. It's all or nothing. Either you want *all* women to be protected and given every opportunity to have success, or you don't. If you don't support the rights of baby girls in the womb, you don't support women's rights.

Abortion not only discards unwanted baby girls as less than garbage but also degrades and harms women in general. Modern feminism's advocacy for abortion "does not value and protect women in their childbearing capacity but seeks to suppress women's bodily functions, using toxic chemicals and deadly devices to violently destroy the life inside her."[15] Defense of abortion, therefore, tells women that they are mere sexual objects, not worth cherishing and raising a family with. This degrading sentiment toward women is compounded by other modern feminist ideals, such as casual sex without commitment.

Who benefits from these modern feminist values? Not women. In addition to being morally wrong and degrading, abortion

---

14 Ibid.

15 Nancy R. Pearcey, *Love Thy Body: Answering Hard Questions about Life and Sexuality* (Grand Rapids, MI: Baker Books, 2018), p. 69

causes significant psychological harm to women. According to a recent meta-analysis study published by the British Journal of Psychiatry, women who had an abortion "experienced an 81% increased risk of mental health problems."[16] Researchers who analyzed data on 877,181 women, of whom 163,831 had an abortion, found that women who experienced an abortion were considerably more likely to develop an anxiety disorder, experience depression, abuse alcohol, and commit suicide—especially when compared to women who carried their pregnancies to term.[17] Casual sex and promiscuity is likewise linked to mental health problems among women. According to a major study of college-aged women in America, "[H]ookup behavior during college was positively correlated with experiencing clinically significant depression symptoms."[18]

In summary, the worldview of modern secular feminism fails to give us any real basis for affirming the moral worth of women and no imperative to protect women. Additionally, the cherished values of secular feminism, such as abortion and casual sex, devalue and harm women. Therefore, modern secular feminism is an obstacle to women's rights, not an effective vehicle for achieving them. The values of secular feminism perpetuate female oppression rather than contribute to female dignity and equality.

---

16   Priscilla K. Coleman, "Abortion and mental health: quantitative synthesis and analysis of research published 1995–2009" *The British Journal of Psychiatry* 199 (2011), p. 180-186

17   Ibid., pp. 181-182

18   Robyn L. Fielder et al., "Sexual Hookups and Abverse Health Outcomes: A Longitudinal Study of First-Year College Women," *The Journal of Sex Research* vol. 51 (2014), quoted in Dennis Prager, The Rational Bible: Exodus (Washington, DC: Regnery, 2018)

Is Christianity Good for Women?

Unlike secular feminism, biblical Christianity provides an objective basis for female dignity and equality. As we covered in chapter one of this book, the overall message of the Bible affirms the immense value and personhood of women. God created both men and women in His image, bestowing upon them intrinsic value and purpose (Genesis 1:27). Women share with men the blessing of dominion over creation (Genesis 1:28). As Davidson puts it, "The fundamental equality of man and woman is unhesitatingly proclaimed in the first chapter of the Bible."[19]

Additionally, the Bible sanctifies sex as a sacred act to be enjoyed only within the marriage covenant, wherein the woman feels honored, protected, and cared for (Genesis 2:24). In the Christian view, women are not objects to be used and discarded. Sex is not to be taken from a woman but lovingly given and shared between husband and wife. Thus, Christianity provides a foundation for men to "do better" in light of the #MeToo movement. God demands that we treat women with respect and protect them against sexual harassment and assault.

It is impossible to deny the positive impact these biblical values have had on women throughout history. As discussed in chapter one, Christianity's sexual ethic, in addition to its opposition to the practices of abortion and infanticide, were among many reasons women in the ancient world were so drawn to the early church.[20] Christianity was also responsible for passing the first laws against sexual slavery, elevating the status of countless oppressed and exploited women in

---

19   Richard M. Davidson, *Flame of Yahweh: Sexuality in the Old Testament* (Peabody, MA: Hendrickson Publishers, 2007), p. 22

20   Nancy R. Pearcey, *Love Thy Body: Answering Hard Questions about Life and Sexuality* (Grand Rapids, MI: Baker Books, 2018), esp. Chapter 2

the ancient world.[21] Historian Kyle Harper writes that "the progressive realization of [the] injustice [of sexual slavery] is a privileged index of Christianization."[22] In other words, sexual slavery being made illegal is one of the surest ways to know that Christianity had thoroughly influenced an ancient society.

While some feminists might be willing to concede the inescapable reality that Christianity has had a positive impact on women's rights throughout history, they still might insist that Christianity *today* is harmful to women. However, the facts demonstrate the opposite. Numerous meta-analysis studies on the social effects of religion have shown that intrinsic religiousness *increases* ethical behavior and overall wellbeing among individuals.

One paper, which looked at various meta-analysis studies conducted in the western world, revealed that religiousness is positively associated with lower rates of crime and delinquency, lower rates of depression, satisfaction with life and happiness, high agreeableness and high conscientiousness, decreased levels of psychoticism, and being respectful, helpful, responsible, and self-disciplined.[23] These positive effects of religion also extend to marriage: "A meta-analytic review of dozens of studies showed that married religious adults are more likely to stay married over time" and have "higher levels of marital satisfaction"[24] Secular feminists often claim that religion is

---

21   Kyle Harper, *From Shame to Sin: The Christian Transformation of Sexual Morality in Late Antiquity* (Cambridge, MA: Harvard University Press, 2013), p. 8

22   Ibid., p. 16, quoted in Nancy R. Pearcey, *Love Thy Body: Answering Hard Questions about Life and Sexuality* (Grand Rapids, MI: Baker Books, 2018)

23   Michael E. McCullough and Brian L. B. Willoughby, "Religion, Self-Regulation, and Self-Control: Associations, Explanations, and Implications," *Psychological Bulletin*, Vol. 135, No. 1 (2009), p. 69-93

24   Ibid., p. 70

"inherently harmful to the human psyche,"[25] yet the scientific data shows us otherwise.

Which Is Better for Women?

As we've established, the modern feminist movement cannot bring about true change in our society. It cannot deliver female dignity and equality. And in fact, some of the highest values of modern feminism (e.g., abortion) are directly contrary to women's rights, worth, and health. Secular feminism cannot solve the problem of female oppression and mistreatment in our society.

So then what *does* work? The answer is biblical Christianity. We know Christianity changes the world and elevates the status of women in society because it already has. Christianity teaches us to value and protect women. Christianity teaches us that women are equal to men in worth and purpose.

Feminism can't change the inward core of humanity, which is ruled by our sinful nature, but the love of Messiah transforms the human heart and compels us to seek justice for the vulnerable. Indeed, Yeshua said that when we care for the "least of these," we are caring for Him. Christianity and the Bible are not the problem; they are the solution. Only the Messiah and His presence within the ministry of the Church can bring about true justice and social change.

---

25 Candace Gorham, "Guilt, Shame, and Psychological Pain," *Women v. Religion: The Case Against Faith—and for Freedom*. Karen L. Garst, ed. (Durham, NC: Pitchstone Publishing, 2018), p. 43

AUTHOR
DAVID WILBER

I am first and foremost a follower of Yeshua the Messiah. I've authored several books, including, *Is God a Misogynist: Understanding the Bible's Difficult Passages Concerning Women*, *When Faith Works: Living Out the Law of Liberty According to James* and *A Christian Guide to the Biblical Feasts*. Additionally, I've written several theological and devotional articles available on various Messianic and Christian websites. I've also spoken at a number of Christian/Messianic churches and conferences throughout the United States and serve as a regular Bible teacher and writer for multiple congregations and ministries, such as 119 Ministries, Founded in Truth Fellowship, and Freedom Hill Community.

One of my passions is to minister to God's people by helping them rediscover the beauty and value of God's Torah. Why? Because Torah observance is an important part of the life and message of our Messiah. It was prophesied that the Messiah would "elevate the Torah and make it honorable" (Isaiah 42:21). The New Covenant established by Yeshua is intended to write the Torah on our hearts through the work of the Holy Spirit (Jeremiah 31:33). Yeshua upheld every dot and iota of the Torah and taught us how to apply it in light of the New Covenant (Matthew 5:17-20). The word *Christian* literally means "follower of Christ." As such, Christians are to walk as Yeshua walked (1 John 2:6). Since Yeshua kept and taught the Torah, it is appropriate for us to do the same.

Another passion of mine is to assist believers in being able to give an answer to anyone who asks about the hope within them (1 Peter 3:15). We are morally responsible to believe, proclaim, and defend the truth and refute falsehoods (Jude 1:3). A branch of theology known as apologetics is devoted to such a task. Therefore, much of my teaching and writing is designed to help believers engage in apologetics so they can confidently answer objections from critics of Christianity and the Bible.

While I certainly don't think of myself as any kind of expert scholar or theologian, I don't believe that God gave me these passions for no reason. And if I can be of service to the body of Messiah, I want to do what I can to help for the glory of God. My plan, therefore, is simply to continue developing resources. In addition to this book, I have a library of articles and videos available for free on my website (www.davidwilber.me). Feel free to connect with me there and on social media. If you'd like to invite me to speak at your congregation or conference, you can contact me through my website.

I hope you were blessed by this book. Thanks for reading. Shalom in the matchless name of Yeshua the Messiah!